More Praise for
*The Decomposition of Man*:
*Identity, Technocracy, and the Church*

"Unlike James Kalb's earlier works, which provide general critiques of liberalism and what Kalb defines as the concept of equal freedom for all, this text is oriented more specifically toward Catholic readers wrestling with the demons of the age. What unites all of Kalb's work, however, is a trenchant investigation of the illusions of late modernity, beginning with the dangerously mistaken belief that individuals can invent their own identities. Kalb's return to the thinking of the High Middle Ages represents a search for a point in Western history before the beliefs that he assails began to take hold."—PAUL GOTTFRIED, author of *Antifascism: The Course of a Crusade*

"In this starkly compelling book, James Kalb demonstrates the inherent contradictions and vacuous assumptions undergirding modern liberal society. For even though our Woke New World remains propped up by immense commercial, technocratic, and bureaucratic might, it can deliver nothing healthy, wholesome, or true. Instead, it merely *manages* people. In this relatively compact work, Kalb *shows us the how and why*. With the precision of a supreme marksman, he zeroes in on the underlying causes. As shot after shot finds its target, a house of cards collapses before our eyes."—ROGER BUCK, author of *The Gentle Traditionalist*

"After articulating the worldview of liberalism or progressivism more comprehensively (and honestly) than its own proponents do, James Kalb systematically dismantles it with deft philosophical argumentation. Shining the light of truth into the chthonic realm of 'egalitarian hedonistic technocracy,' Kalb vindicates the irreplaceable role of natural and traditional sources of identity and purpose, including a person's sex, family commitments, culture, and religion. Simply masterful."—PETER A. KWASNIEWSKI, author of *The Ecstasy of Love in the Thought of Thomas Aquinas*

"'Industrialization,' James Kalb argues, is 'dehumanizing and to all appearances cannot stop being so.' Quoting Emerson's insight that it means 'things are in the saddle and ride mankind,' Kalb explores its deracinating and destabilizing role in the decline of the West. This is a bracing book about the dangers of severing man's intellect from his labor. It also exposes the futility of the leisure state's dependence on the liberal vision of human nature as essentially uncorrupted. Although Kalb offers no easy solution, 'the future,' he reminds us, 'belongs to those who accept the truth about man and the nature of things.'"—WILL KNOWLAND, Former Master at Eton College

# The Decomposition of Man
*Identity, Technocracy, and the Church*

JAMES KALB

# The Decomposition of Man

*Identity,
Technocracy,
and the Church*

Angelico Press

First published by Angelico Press, 2023
© James Kalb, 2023

All rights reserved

No part of this book may be reproduced or transmitted,
in any form or by any means, without permission.

For information, address:
Angelico Press
169 Monitor St.
Brooklyn, NY 11222
www.angelicopress.com

978-1-62138-922-4 paperback
978-1-62138-923-1 cloth
978-1-62138-924-8 ebook

Cover Design: Michael Schrauzer

# CONTENTS

## PART I: The Disintegration of Identity

### 1 Introduction • 1

### 2 Identity as a Problem • 5
Novelty of situation—Traditional understandings—How they worked—Variations—The question of justice

### 3 The Attack on Functional Identities • 13
Sexual identities—American and Western identity—Their state today—Why they matter—How they have changed—Seeming inconsistencies

### 4 The Aggressiveness of the Attack • 23
Tyrannical tolerance—Bigoted inclusiveness—Examples

### 5 Intellectual Background • 29
Ruling class madness—Industrialized thought—Technocratic ideals—Metaphysical confusion—Shrunken horizons—Scientism—Subjectivism

### 6 Practical Background • 41
Historical—Economic—Industrial society—A mechanical world—Tyranny as liberation

## PART II: A World Transformed

### 7 Social Consequences • 53
End of boundaries—Human ties dissolve—Life comes unglued—Institutional wreckage—End of thought—Failed meritocracy—Growing ineffectuality—Resulting blindness—No place for thought

### 8 Human Realities • 62
Daily life—A new morality—Totalitarian liberation—Unequal equality—Servile freedom—Illiberal education

### 9 Political Correctness • 69
Nature—Effects—PC culture—The great awokening—Tyranny rising—Coolness

### 10 A New Order? • 81
Progressivism as a faith—Its strengths—Its weaknesses—The new identities—Their failure—Identity politics

### 11 Political Paralysis • 90
Triumph of the strong—Fascism—Progressivism—Similarities—Progressivism and power—Conservatism—Maintaining continuity—Restraints on "progress"—Social conservatism—Religious and intellectual conservatism—Awkwardness about identity—Other rightist tendencies

### 12 Downfall • 105
Petrifaction—A simplified world—Flawed rebellions—Alternatives abandoned—Practical entrenchment—Self-destruction—Insoluble problems—The coming crash—What follows?

## PART III: A New Foundation

### 13 Changing Course • 117

Taking a stand—Contesting liberalism—False account of man—False freedom and equality—Essential inhumanity—The antimodern alternative—Views new and old—Putting the question—Making the case

### 14 Nature • 130

What is natural law?—Sex—Political role—Social setting—Social justice—Nation—Particularism—Nationalism—Cosmopolitanism

### 15 Tradition • 141

What tradition is—Authority—Paradox of traditionalism—Objections—Development—Growth—Decline—American tradition

### 16 The Church • 154

Beyond tradition—Faith—Religion—Christianity—Catholicism

## PART IV: Turning Around

### 17 A Choice, Not an Echo • 163

Individual commitment—Difficulties—The power of example—Dangers of assimilation—Distinctiveness—Benedict of Nursia—Variants—How it grows

## 18 Objections • 175

Turning inward—The Church and the world—Separation and engagement—Benefits of monasticism—Exclusion—Objection—Response—Lurking problems

## 19 Challenges • 187

Legal—Social—Economic—Educational—Intellectual—Spiritual—Gradual decay

## 20 Outlook • 198

## Bibliography • 204

# PART I

The Disintegration of Identity

# 1

# Introduction

In 2008 I published a book, *The Tyranny of Liberalism*, arguing that equal freedom defeats itself when it is taken as the first principle of political life. In 2013 I published another, *Against Inclusiveness*, analyzing liberal society, and arguing that the real meaning of "inclusiveness," an ideal now considered beyond criticism, is the destruction of all serious social connections that cannot be reduced to money or bureaucracy. This book explores an aspect of that destruction, the suppression of traditional understandings of human identity.

What is man, and who is this particular man? Nothing very definite, we are now told: the habit of classifying human beings, even the concept of "human nature," is oppressive. But that means that when we deal with people we cannot be guided by what they are as human beings or the particular kind of people they are. We must consider them from some other perspective—perhaps as the creators of who they are, or alternatively as resources for the projects of others. We are marching into a post-human future in which man, depending on point of view, is either a god or less than a beast.

And we are indeed marching—or being marched. For all the talk of diversity, politics today is extraordinarily uniform. The West lives under a single political regime, managerial liberalism, that integrates the interests of commercial and bureaucratic elites. In the past the conflict between money and bureaucracy as ruling principles—capitalism and socialism—was basic to much of Western politics. However, the collapse of socialism, professionalization of business management, and growth of the regulatory and welfare state have convinced businessmen and bureaucrats alike that they do best in a system in which they manage social relations and the economy jointly in the interests of prosperity and stability. That arrangement serves the interests and outlook of both sides of the partnership, and is unlikely to be seriously disturbed by the dreams of libertarians or leftists to eliminate one side or the other or to change its basic goals.

The result has been a system that combines idealization of equality and individual choice with domination of social life by experts, functionaries, and commercial interests. The liberal and managerial aspects of this system seem at odds with each other, but both are fundamental to it and they work together surprisingly well. The people who run it view the principles of freedom, equality, and efficiency as the uniquely rational goals for social order. That view has led to an attempt to reconstruct social life to make it align with those principles through and through, using the legal and administrative means now considered the natural vehicle for rational public action. Bureaucrats are to remake us and our relations with each other so we become free and equal on the dimensions now thought to define what is important in life—that is, as consumers, people with careers, and recipients of various forms of social assistance. Otherwise, it is said, some will be excluded from activities and social connections now considered central to human life, and thus denied status as full human beings.

As a result, only the commercial and bureaucratic institutions that define the system can be allowed to affect our social existence. The aspects of identity that order traditional arrangements, such as family, religion, and inherited cultural community, must therefore be made as voluntary, subject to personal interpretation, and practically insignificant as possible, and so in effect abolished. Otherwise, non-commercial and non-bureaucratic considerations will affect social position and rewards and thus produce inequalities: mothers, for example, will not have the same career success as fathers, and those of French ancestry will have an advantage in French society over those of Sub-Saharan heritage.

However odd this belief in liberation through careerism, consumerism, and comprehensive bureaucratic control may be, it is

## Introduction

accepted without question, and has led to suppression of principles that are as basic as the distinction between the sexes. Even a legal and philosophical concept like citizenship is suspect, since it has to do with particular connections and loyalties.[1] So it too needs to be made irrelevant to everything that matters: borders must be opened, voting rights granted to non-citizens, and so on.

Educated and responsible people take the resulting social ideal for granted and view any other as inconceivable and indeed evil. No one respectable can imagine a future, apart from violence, chaos, and tyranny, that is anything but more of the same, and those who oppose such a future are considered malicious, out of touch, or psychologically disordered. If you are skeptical about affirmative action or transgenderism, do not trust "the experts," or complain about rule by de-nationalized billionaires and bureaucrats—concretely, if you supported Trump, Brexit, or even the mildest of Republicans, or you doubted some feature of your local COVID regime—there is something seriously wrong with you. And if there are many who share your views, they are a serious threat to human decency and public order that must urgently be dealt with.

However many intelligent, informed, and responsible people accept this social ideal, they are wrong. Human beings cannot be stripped of all qualities other than those relevant to their status as components of a global economic machine. The problem is not a specific error in fact, judgment, or policy that our rulers might rectify if a critic pointed it out. Nor is it a temporary excess. Instead, it is a problem with the technological outlook that dominates public thought today, and thus with views of knowledge and rational action that have achieved absolute dominance because they aid our rulers in what they care about—the acquisition of wealth and power. These views are grossly inadequate for understanding human beings or ordering life in general, but they have long led to military and economic success, and the more single-mindedly such success is emphasized the more uniquely rational the underlying worldview is thought to be.

---

1 See Dimitry Kochenov, "Why We Shall Abolish Citizenship."

Even so, such views eventually become destructive, because they leave out important realities. But the more detached from reality they become, the more difficult they are to oppose. How can you argue with people who are detached from reality when they effectively monopolize positions of social and intellectual authority, and to all appearances the very ability to understand alternative perspectives has been trained out of them? The great political question today is what to do about such a situation. No political or social issue can be dealt with rationally until we recover our collective grip on reality. The purpose of this book is to understand how that might be done, and to that end it explores the historical, intellectual, and institutional influences that have led to our present situation, and what ways are open to us to counteract them and build something better.

This book is written from a Catholic point of view because I consider Catholicism the most comprehensively true and useful view of man and the world. Its final conclusions are also Catholic. Our current problems go too deep for anything less to serve. Even so, the general analysis and specific arguments do not depend on Catholic doctrine, so they ought to be accessible to non-Catholics and non-Christians.

Catholic social and moral doctrine is mostly a matter of natural law—of human nature, natural human goods, and the normal healthy functioning of society—and those are the grounds upon which I will argue. The function of Catholicism in this regard is to provide a practical way for natural law to become stable and binding, and so more than theory.

The Catholic Faith of course has importance beyond social and political matters. It would not be socially useful if it did not precede and go beyond what is social. In the final part of the book, where I discuss how to work toward a better world, I discuss that and other aspects of the need to emphasize ultimate truths regarding God, man, and the world. Man is dependent as well as autonomous; there is no substitute for reality; and a society that forgets these things goes mad. But everything in order.

# 2

# Identity as a Problem

Personal and social identity have become problems. No one seems to know what they are, where they come from, what they are for, or what difference they should make. The question is not just who gets classified how, or the situation and common concerns of this group or that, but the nature of identity as such. People think it is enormously important. It defines who we are, and the individual right to decide that question is now thought absolutely fundamental. So if a man declares himself a woman his birth certificate must be altered to say he is female, and if a male weightlifter identifies as a woman he may compete as such.

This alleged right deprives identity of content by allowing people to define it however they want. Even so, it is taken very seriously. To deny someone's self-chosen identity is considered an attempt to destroy him as what he is, and thus almost murder; at the very least, it is to treat him as less than human by denying his right of self-definition. If you are willing to do that, people believe, there is no limit to what you might do to him. So it is increasingly enforced legally, and feminists who object to it on the grounds that it dissolves the distinctive identity of actual women are declared "trans exclusionary" and expelled from decent progressive company.

### Novelty of situation

This is an unprecedented situation. In the past, sane people knew and accepted who they were, certainly with regard to something as basic as sex, and it did not occur to them to do otherwise. A confident sense of one's identity and place in the world was considered an obvious good. It preceded choice, because it gave people a perspective from which they could understand and deal with life coherently. And it was basic to self-respect, because it enabled people to know and stand their ground.

These features of identity depended on its stability and objectivity. To say identity was stable and objective is not to say it was permanently fixed in all its details. Office, a ruler's favor, or an advantageous marriage could raise someone in the social scale. Age, wealth, accomplishments, and personal character would eventually tell. Disgrace could lead to loss of status. And, in spite of the general dislike of pretense, social climbing might have some effect. But such changes were limited, required cooperation from others, and were usually slow, so that the rise or decline of a family in social class might take generations. People did not see identity as something chosen or created, and someone who treated it that way was an impostor or madman.

Under such circumstances identity did not come up as a serious problem, except in connection with religious or philosophical speculations. Christians might say that personal identity had to do with the immortal soul, Buddhists and Taoists that it was an illusion, Kant that it was an awareness of the unified functioning of the mind. The Muslims would no doubt subject it to the infinite arbitrary power of God—hence the dreamlike quality and wild swings of fortune found in the *Arabian Nights*. But as a practical matter no one doubted whether he was a man or woman; only in unusual cases could he doubt whether he was married or unmarried, a Scot or a Spaniard; and it was almost always sufficiently clear what those things meant. Today all that has changed, at least in theory and increasingly in practice. We are constantly told—and many have come to believe—that the differences between the sexes are minimal and should not matter, and if a man says he is a woman he really is a woman.[1] Few people really doubt their correct sex, but there are getting to be more of them—especially among impressionable young girls[2]—and

---

1 Stoyan Zaimov, "4 in 10 Americans Say Gender Is Not Determined at Birth: Survey."

2 See Abigail Shrier, *Irreversible Damage: The Transgender Craze Seducing Our Daughters* and Jeffrey M. Jones, "LGBT Identification in U.S. Ticks up to 7.1%."

*Identity as a Problem*

those who are put off when a man or woman fails to act like a man or woman are now considered hopeless deplorables.

But what does all this mean? If sexual distinctions are too fluid and unimportant to attend to, why is it important to view a man who says he is a woman as a woman? What does it mean to do so? If something that has always—for good reason—been considered basic to human life can be transformed at will, is there anything in human life that is stable and determinate enough to be understood at all? And why is it "hate" to view current claims as nonsensical?

## Traditional understandings

It may be helpful to discuss a concrete example of identity as traditionally understood, and as it still tends to be understood where people are not constantly indoctrinated.

To choose an example close to hand—myself—I am a human being; a man, son, brother, husband, and father; a Catholic, Westerner, and American. So I belong to a particular species, sex, family, Church, civilization, and country. These characteristics are part of what I am, and I cannot undo any of them easily or in most cases at all. I cannot drop out of the human race, unman myself, disown my blood relations, undo my baptism, or unmarry myself.[3] I acquired some of these characteristics involuntarily, others through my actions, the response of others, and the nature of the case. I had no choice becoming a human being, son, brother, or American. Nor could I choose my children, although I could have avoided becoming a father. In a sense I had more choice becoming a Catholic, since I am a convert, but my conversion was less a choice than acceptance that I had already become Catholic in outlook and loyalty. To remain outside the Church would have been to ignore recognitions and connections that were becoming ever more central to how I understood myself and the world. That would have been less a choice than a lie. And while I could theoretically apostatize, for me that is a purely logical possibility, like becoming a flat-earther.

---

3  As I said, I am Catholic. More basically, I cannot understand how it is easier to say "this woman is no longer my wife" than "this woman is no longer my sister."

Getting married might seem more a matter of simple choice. It is less likely that there is One True Bride than One True Church, so I could have married or not in good conscience. But marriage also involved dispositions that are not simply a matter of choice, such as a settled desire to join my life irrevocably to that of another person—not to mention acceptance by that other. And, of course, becoming Catholic and getting married required the existence of the Church and of marriage, institutions I did not and could not possibly create.

### How they worked

These identities are social as well as individual. They make me what I am, and also place me in society. The two are connected, since how I understand myself, my good, the world and my place in it, what I am and what I should do and be, depends largely on social networks to which I belong. The most important of these, almost by definition, relate to aspects of identity: if a network is sufficiently fundamental to my life, my position in it helps define who I am.

Man is a rational animal, and part of this is that he bases what he should do on his conception of what he and others are. Personal and social identity tell us who we are, what that means, and what we owe to others and can expect from them. That helps us think coherently about what to do, and tells others how to deal with us. For that reason personal and social identity have always accounted for much of the institutional aspect of society, the differentiated positions and responsibilities that are necessary for it to function. Consider, for example, men, women, and their union in marriage that has been the basis of social order throughout history. Men and women do not remain true to each other and look loyally after their families because of impulse, incentives, penalties, or contractual obligations. Nor is it purely instinctive. They do so mostly because of how they understand themselves, their connections to others, and the duties associated with those things. They are husbands and wives, fathers and mothers. Those things are fundamental to their understanding of who they are, and they act accordingly. Or consider religious identity, Catholicism in Europe for example, which served as the integrating principle of what became the civilization of the West through its definition of social identities from marriage to kingship, and its connection of those things to fundamental reality. To violate one's duty in such a system was not simply to break a social rule: it was to act falsely, to deny what one was and thus to betray oneself.

A well-functioning system of identities is thus basic to a normal and rewarding way of life. It brings with it a system of understandings, practices, obligations, and ideals that durably relates us functionally to others, and gives us a perspective from which we can reason effectively about our lives and place in the world. People recognize tradition and culture as basic to human life. But tradition and culture are always interwoven with a system of identities. So the latter is part of what makes human life organized and functional, and us social and rational.

## Variations

The personal and social nature of identity means that understandings of identity—of what it is to be a human being, man, Catholic, or member of a family, what I should do as such, and so on—differ somewhat among Tom, Dick, and Harry, and among Americans, Italians, and Japanese. Even so, identity is no more a pure social construction than it is a personal invention. Some version of basic aspects of human identity, some understanding of humanity, blood relationship, marriage, sexual distinctions and roles, and our place with regard to ultimate reality, is basic to every society and thus—since these versions have a great deal in common—to the constitution of human life. We can read ancient, medieval, or Eastern literature and recognize men, women, and families that are fundamentally similar to our own.

The similarities show that some versions of identity fit human nature better than others. Culture builds on natural realities like the distinction between male and female and the relation between parents and children, and shapes how we deal with them, but it does not make or unmake them. It declares whether horse flesh should be eaten, but it cannot tell us dirt should— even though some people eat it—and it is unlikely to keep people who are generally meat-eaters from eating horse flesh when starving. A similar situation applies in other aspects of life. Nature tells us, for example, that there are two sexes, they differ deeply, and one cannot be turned into the other. How people respond to that has varied by time, place, social class, and so on. Can a man divorce his wife or take a concubine? Answers were different in traditional England and traditional Japan. Even so, basic patterns are obvious. Recognizing a functional distinction between the sexes, with men playing a more public and women a more domestic role, is a human universal.

Differences such as men's greater physical strength and concern for abstract function, and women's greater concern for amenity and specific human relationships, provide much of the basis for such distinctions. These differences are evidently innate: social scientists find that sex differences in personality and occupational choice are actually greater in countries that promote sexual equality[4]—when people are told to do what they want, their choices are usually stereotypical. With that in mind, we can be confident that systems of the traditional kind, which give form to natural tendencies and make use of them, work better than the unisex or radically egalitarian multigender systems now enforced as a requirement of reason and justice. Recognizing marriage as a relationship between man and woman, and the obligations of husband and wife as specific, complementary, durable, and grounded in the nature of things—and thus oriented toward procreation and the rearing of children—leads to marriages that are more stable, functional, and satisfying to those involved than treating them as purely contractual, endlessly changeable, terminable at will, or subject to an overriding principle of absolute equality, let alone abandoning institutional form altogether in favor of a shapeless system of "relationships," "gender identities," and "hooking up."

## The question of justice

Even so, many consider stable systems of identity unjust. After all, these tell people what to do, and put some above others in the

---

[4] See, e.g., David P. Schmitt et al., "Why Can't a Man Be More Like a Woman? Sex Differences in Big Five Personality Traits Across 55 Cultures."

social scale. Not everyone is satisfied with his position, the distinctions sometimes seem arbitrary, and advantages are sometimes abused. But traditional distinctions are not the only ones that can be invidious. The same objections apply to private property and to institutional position and status, which also distinguish, discriminate, exclude, and compel in ways that often seem arbitrary and arouse resentment.

We can always speculate about who truly deserves what, and complain about the way property is apportioned, people appointed to positions, and identities assigned and defined. Even so, doing away with private property, organizational structures, or stable social identities because of real or imagined flaws in actual arrangements would cause far more problems than it would solve. Such systems are always imperfect, but they would not exist unless they were better than random choice as a way of assigning responsibilities to people. More importantly, they are essential for peaceful and orderly cooperation, and have the indispensable virtue of giving people something of their own that enables them to determine what makes sense in their relations with others. The alternative is a world of open-ended self-definition, self-seeking, aggression, and mutual exploitation. The question is not whether social arrangements distinguish, discriminate, exclude, and compel—they always do, sometimes unfairly—but whether they promote a way of life worth living. Traditional social identities and the arrangements they support give a place in social life to considerations—human nature, love and loyalty, the psychological security of children, the Good, Beautiful, and True—that cannot be translated into commercial or bureaucratic terms or made a matter of individual consumer or lifestyle choice. That is enough to justify them.

They also create inequalities that can sometimes seem unjust, but so do all institutions, notoriously including the bureaucratic and commercial institutions basic to a liberal and progressive social order. A general remedy is impossible. It would require an authority capable of arranging a remedy for every inequality that seems unjust, and that would not work as intended. Apart from the difficulty of finding the truth and determining what is fair in every case, it would require an enormous, even unlimited power over the entire social order. Those who hold it could use that power to tyrannize over everything at will, and why expect it to be exercised justly? In any event, its ability to redefine our identity would destroy our own ability to know securely who we are and where we stand with regard to others, and so create a new dependence on the central authority. That would leave us with no settled social position of any sort, and in no position to resist whatever is demanded of us. Why consider that liberating?

# 3

# The Attack on Functional Identities

America and the West are in the midst of a comprehensive identity crisis, one that seems to dissolve all identities even as—paradoxically but inevitably—these are obsessively emphasized. One aspect of this crisis is that traditional dimensions of identity are under attack by major social institutions.

## Sexual identities

At the moment, the attack on sexual identity that we have been discussing is the most prominent manifestation of the crisis. Complementary physical and behavioral differences between male and female have been basic to all human societies, and have existed among the higher animals for hundreds of millions of years. In our time they have nonetheless dissolved as accepted reality in the case of human beings. As a result, every difference in nature, tendency, or role between men and women is challenged or rejected outright. There are exceptions to the extent that women are thought to have special strengths and competencies, or they seem to require special protection against masculine aggression and physical strength,[1] but otherwise the sexes are generally proclaimed to be indistinguishable.

Even so, it is considered supremely important to accept the person who became famous as Bruce Jenner for his triumphs as a male athlete as a woman named Caitlyn, because that is who he

[1] As in the case of athletics, in which women are protected from male competition, and women's "safe spaces," from which men are excluded for reasons of "safety"—a need that is very broadly construed. The situation has become somewhat complicated with the rise of transgenderism.

says he is. And if tomorrow he says he is neither male nor female, but something else, and his pronouns are "xe" and "xir," we will have to go along with that too on pain (in New York City) of a possible $250,000 fine for repeated infractions.[2] How the compulsion to deny that womanhood means anything at all in the case of ordinary women is to be reconciled with the compulsion to accept its reality and importance in Jenner's case is left unclear. What can its content and significance be in his case when the bedrock social principle is that it means nothing whatever? Do we have to ask him, along with each of the millions of other "transgender" people, and follow in each case whatever their individual and possibly changing understandings of the matter may be? The multiplicity of "genders" and new rules growing up around the use of pronouns suggests that may be the case.

### American and Western identity

But the dissolution of settled forms of identity comprehends far more than sex. At a more general level it includes cultural identity, which once provided a scheme within which other aspects of identity could find their place.

American and Western identity provide an example. These are historical developments rather than human universals, natural facts, or divinely ordained realities. In the time of Christ neither existed; people who possess them are now a shrinking minority in the world, and some day they will no longer exist. Even so, they are not spurious or insignificant. America and the West have long and distinctive histories, function to some extent as wholes, and have given rise to immensely valuable traditions of thought, inquiry, art, devotion, government, and social life. To continue with myself as an example, growing up in them marked me indelibly, and brought with it obligations toward the people, ideas, and institutions that helped make me what I am. I am distinctly American and Western.

---

2 Dan Evon, "New NYC Laws Prohibit Discrimination against Transgender Community." The same penalty applies to calling an alien an alien. Bailey Vogt, "NYC Bans Calling Someone an 'Illegal Alien' or Threatening to Contact ICE."

## Their state today

On the other hand, America and the West have changed a great deal during my life, along with the principles and spirit that animate them. Their rulers have been guiding them more and more decisively toward open borders and inclusion of what was formerly viewed as non-American and non-Western. These changes are replacing American and Western identity with a radical cosmopolitanism, but to oppose them is now considered a betrayal of American and Western values and even identity. "That is not who we are," as President Obama was fond of saying.[3] So America and the West have turned against themselves. This has gone to extremes in the "woke" movement that grew up in the past decade and really exploded after the death of George Floyd, with major institutions signing on to the theory that whites and "whiteness," and thus the Western heritage, are uniquely destructive forces that need urgently to be suppressed by any means necessary. The result is that any appeal to specifically Western or American tradition, for example speaking of sheriffs as part of the "Anglo-American heritage of law enforcement,"[4] is now considered a "white supremacist" attack on American ideals. To be traditionally American, then, has come to be understood as anti-American, and similar tendencies are visible in other Western countries. "Western values" are thought to include an increasingly radical universalism.

It is doubtful that populist rebellions such as Brexit or the Trump movement will change any of this. The uniform failure of populist uprisings, their lack of institutional and intellectual depth, the absence of a clear vision of a better world, the opposition of elites, and the strength of the tendencies that have led us where we are make fundamental reversal unlikely without radical crisis. The very insanity of a program of national and civilizational dissolution and the hysterical reaction among educated and responsible people to recent events that reveal widespread

---

[3] David Rutz, "46 Times President Obama Told Americans 'That's Not Who We Are.'"

[4] See, for example, Marwa Eltagouri, "Jeff Sessions Spoke of the 'Anglo-American Heritage of Law Enforcement.' Here's What That Means."

doubts about it confirm the difficulty of opposing the program, since they underline the strength of liberal trends among those who run our world and their immunity to considerations of reason, advantage, and popular sentiment.

## Why they matter

And that presents a very serious problem. American and Western identities may be dispensable in a sense—life went on for people living in Athens and Rome after the disappearance of classical civilization, although the population of Rome dropped sharply—but membership in a particular people and affiliation with a particular civilization is needed for a humane system of social cooperation and a stable and functional self-understanding. So the self-destruction of the world's dominant and historically most productive civilization is likely to lead to very little good and a great deal of evil.

A people is a population joined by common history, institutions, loyalties, and ways of living, and a sense of common destiny, while a civilization is a complex of peoples joined by a larger history that has given rise to common aspirations and understandings. Such things are no doubt a matter of degree and to some extent based on arbitrary line-drawing. Are Italians a people? If so, are Sicilians and Sardinians part of that people? The Italian Swiss? Where do the South Tyrolese or the Jews who have been living in Italy since Roman times fit in? Peoples, nations, and civilizations nonetheless exist and matter, just as families, extended families, neighborhoods, social classes, circles of friends, and political and social movements exist and matter. The definition and boundaries of all these things can be debated, and they change over time, but their existence and importance cannot be doubted if we want to understand human life. In their varying ways such groupings provide members with more or less coherent common frameworks for living that include common loyalties and the common habits, attitudes, and understandings that add up to culture. The universal importance of such things is part of what it means to say that man is social.

The culture of a people functions in large part by recognizing the various aspects of identity and giving them a common interpretation so that people's lives together can be coherent, productive, and rewarding. It tells us what we are so we will know how to understand ourselves, each other, and the world around us, and what to do about the situations in which we find ourselves. So a culture normally includes a somewhat coherent common understanding of masculinity, femininity, family relations, religion, and human things in general, and attributes an importance to those things related to their natural function. These understandings and other aspects of a people's culture and way of life develop over time and work together to create a system that may have idiosyncrasies but makes sense as a whole. For example, peoples with less developed public institutions are likely to have a stronger feeling for family, extended family, and the distinction between the sexes, since fewer responsibilities for one kind of institution mean more responsibilities for others and thus a greater emphasis on the social distinctions that support them.

## How they have changed

Until recently, American culture, and that of the broader West, followed that normal human pattern. Like other cultures, these had flaws as well as strengths, but they gave their people something to work with and a setting in which they could carry on their lives in ways that made sense to them. And they gave rise to glorious achievements that have permanently benefited humanity—in the case of the West broadly defined to include its roots in Athens, Rome, and Jerusalem, more than any other culture ever. The spread of Western culture through the world, like the spread of Greek culture through the Middle East and Central Asia beginning in the fourth century BC, and the enduring authority of Roman culture and institutions throughout the European Middle Ages, was due partially to military success but mostly to Westerners' own belief in its superiority, a belief that was often accepted even outside the West. Without such a belief and its widespread acceptance by others, the fate of Western culture outside Western Europe, Greek culture in the lands conquered by Alexander, and Latin culture in the lands of the Western Roman Empire would have been like the fate of Mongol culture in the lands conquered by Genghis Khan.

Today the situation is changing, in part because of the very success of the West. What developed most, spread most, and acquired the most influence was what could be most easily reproduced—not the heritage of Christendom, but the most abstract and universalizing features of the modern West, such as technology, industrialization, an anti-traditional spirit, and acceptance of efficiency and equality as guiding principles. The result has been a worldwide tendency for traditional arrangements to be replaced by bureaucratic social administration and the cash nexus. This tendency toward an industrial form of society has seemingly become irresistible as social life becomes globally more integrated.

The tendency has been strongest in the West itself, where a principle of technologically rational social organization is realized by turning people into interchangeable parts through mass schooling, including mass higher education, an emphasis on formal qualifications, and a determined effort to root out distinctions related to traditional aspects of identity. The latter reflect local particularities, and deal with aspects of life that cannot be mechanized and have little relevance to the aspects of social functioning our rulers care about. The response to them is to make them as voluntary, subject to personal interpretation, and practically insignificant as possible. Instances of particularity that seem indispensable, for example obligations between parents and children, and national citizenship with its rights and obligations, are dealt with by viewing them as creations of the law that can and should be changed whenever social policy demands, and whose effects should be minimized.

The success of the West has thus meant its self-destruction, since all principles and institutions that cannot be reduced to the general principles of a technological society have come to be viewed as arbitrary and oppressive, or at best as individual preferences that must not be allowed to affect others. The result is that people now believe that a "genderqueer" Somali atheist living in a small Ohio town should, in his own as well as others' judgment, have the same respect, acceptance, opportunities, and likelihood of success as anyone else. If he suffers some disadvantage because he falls outside local networks of inherited connections or his way of life violates traditional local standards and culture, that is an injustice that must be rectified. And if his self-understood identity is not fully accepted, celebrated, and included in all settings, he is being deprived of recognition as a full human being and is thus a victim. How then can the people victimizing him by failing to make him feel included—the people who had been living peacefully, cooperatively, and productively in the town before he showed up—complain if he lashes out?

Such principles are now thought to be a matter of basic human decency. Even the many people who do not accept them through and through cannot argue against them, since the logic of public discussion—which, as we shall see, is based on an ever more radical version of liberal modernity—gives them no way to do so. So proponents of the new principles win arguments, and are radically transforming society with no end in sight.

## Seeming inconsistencies

Some situations suggest limitations to the fluidity and subjectivity of identity that can be insisted on. A woman named Rachel Dolezal, who had built a career on her claim to be black, made national news, and lost her positions with civic, journalistic, and academic organizations, when it emerged that she was of unmixed Northern and Central European ancestry. Growing up in a racially mixed family, and identifying with her black adoptive brothers, was not enough to allow her to identify as black.[5] There have been a number of similar incidents involving people—mostly female academics—who claim American Indian ancestry. Other limits are suggested by objections to "cultural appropriation," which involves white people adopting a motif, symbol, or practice from a culture not ancestrally their own.

Progressives generally oppose Miss Dolezal's self-identification as black, and cultural appropriation in general. The opposition seems surprising, since it presumes the legitimacy of racial and cultural boundaries that exclude outsiders. Even more surprisingly, the contrast with transgenderism suggests that progressives believe that race and even culture are more fixed than sex, a

[5] Decca Aitkenhead, "Rachel Dolezal: 'I'm Not Going to Stoop and Apologise and Grovel.'"

distinction that is incomparably more ancient, fundamental, and well-defined. Progressives explain the latter discrepancy by speaking of "gender," which they say is a socially constructed or personally chosen category with no necessary relation to "sex," which is biological. But even if the distinction is accepted, it is not clear why gender should be treated as more fluid than race or culture, since progressives insist that these too are constructions. And they do not consistently accept the distinction themselves, since they insist that transgender people should be classified medically—and therefore biologically—in accordance with their chosen identity, thus dissolving biological sex as a distinct category.[6] That is the point of transgenderism: a "trans woman," people insist, is simply a woman.

The contrast between treatment of transgenderism and treatment of transracialism, cultural appropriation, and so on is not principled, but it can be understood strategically as part of the overall progressive campaign against traditional identities. Disrupting the function and significance of identities relating to sex, kinship, ethnicity, religion, and culture is basic to that campaign. The most obvious way of disrupting them is to emphasize the oppressiveness of dominant identities and insist on their suppression as a matter of justice or even defense against "violence." Thus, the presence of non-Christian religions means Christmas can no longer be a public celebration because that would assign non-Christians a lesser value. And slavery and the black experience mean that all American history is tainted forever.[7] Nothing from the dominant American tradition can be treated as legitimate other than the aspects that have led to contemporary progressivism—that is, the aspects that are leading to the dissolution of the tradition as a whole. Anything, like Black Lives Matter, that sharpens opposition to that tradition is therefore favored no matter how much rioting or how many murders it leads to.[8]

---

6 See "US Proposal for Defining Gender Has No Basis in Science."

7 See "The 1619 Project," *The New York Times Magazine*, August 14, 2019.

8 For the consequences of the Black Lives Matter movement, see Wilfred Reilly, Robert Maranto, and Patrick Wolf, "Did Black Lives Matter Save Black Lives?," and Scott Alexander, "What Caused the 2020 Homicide Spike?"

## The Attack on Functional Identities

But another way to suppress traditionally dominant identities, as in Miss Dolezal's case, is to dissolve them by denying their distinctiveness and emphasizing that of others. So "whiteness" is purely a construction: the Irish are said to have been non-white before they were socially declared otherwise.[9] "Black," in contrast, is treated as a genuine identity with real content. That is why it is capitalized by the *Associated Press Stylebook* while "white" is not, and it is why Miss Dolezal did not become black when she said she was. And it is also why cultural appropriation of blackness and other non-dominant traditions is opposed as reactionary—it reduces the indigestible angularity that keeps them from blending into the traditions of the mainstream basically white culture.

With regard to transgenderism, different circumstances require different responses. Like "whiteness," "masculinity" cannot be allowed to denote a natural reality. The multiplicity of racial and ethnic groupings make it possible to abolish whiteness without abolishing Blackness, for example by treating whiteness as an arbitrary assemblage of tendencies from a variety of sources. In contrast, the binary nature of sexuality means masculinity cannot be abolished while femininity remains. That is why all implications of transgenderism, unlike those of transracialism, must be accepted without reservation. If getting rid of women is the price of getting rid of men, that is what must be done. The ultimate point, after all, is not to do anything for women—or for that matter, for blacks—but to abolish the relevance of all such concepts to social functioning. Even currently promoted identities like "Black" and "transgender" are not intended to serve any function other than opposition to the identities traditionally dominant. The implicit goal—that is, the goal actually served, even if not consciously held, and supported by class and institutional interests—is for disembodied and ahistorical influences like money and bureaucracy to be the only legitimate principles of social order. Other influences mean "privilege," and so are bigoted and discriminatory.

---

9  Noel Ignatiev, *How the Irish Became White*.

This outlook is now accepted by all significant public institutions. It is considered liberating, even though it destroys the reliability of human connections other than bureaucracy and the cash nexus, and thus means billionaires and bureaucrats end up running everything. But more on that in later chapters.

# 4

# The Aggressiveness of the Attack

What is described above constitutes an unprecedented attack by a ruling class on its own people and their way of life. But no one knows how to say so coherently and effectively in the language of today's mainstream public discussion, so people submit—if not all at once, then bit by bit and then ever faster.

## Tyrannical tolerance

For people who retain a somewhat traditional view of things, the most striking feature of the current situation is its astounding intolerance. For our rulers these issues are beyond discussion. Everyone must agree with what they tell us, and those who do not are worthy only of contempt.

An obvious result has been a radical narrowing of public discussion. It is acceptable to be socialist and even somewhat acceptable to be libertarian or communist. These distinctions have to do with the relative role of markets, bureaucracies, and private property in today's social order. In purely economic matters, to err one way or the other just means you are somewhat softer or harder than you should be, or perhaps a bit unrealistic. Such tolerance does not apply to any view that recognizes the social authority of tradition, religion, sexual distinctions, inherited community, or natural law. Progressives reject the social function of such things, and view them as non-rational private tastes to be pursued only as individual hobbies or consumption choices, and then only when they do not affect other people. To treat them as authoritative, they believe, even as a matter of informal social attitudes, would be to impose arbitrary demands by force. And that they view as the essence of fascism.

So any view that opposes the regnant subjectivism—for example, regarding male and female as fixed categories, or marriage as a specific natural arrangement with intrinsic goals and functions rather than an aggregate of free-form personal projects—is seen as a bigoted assertion of "privilege." If you oppose "gay marriage," the explanation is not that you recognize natural marriage—the physical, social, and spiritual union of man and woman for mutual support, procreation, and the rearing of children—as a universal fundamental human institution that deserves recognition and support as such. That explanation is incomprehensible to our rulers, who reject natural and traditional forms in favor of social policy based on technological ways of thinking as a way to order human life. Instead, they believe that you must have an irrational animus against those attracted to people of the same sex.[1] You want to deny them human connections that are basic to their self-definition and thus, since man is the being that defines himself, to their human essence.

That denial is considered an attempt to "erase" them and so annihilate a whole class of people. Natural and traditional views regarding identity are said to demonstrate ignorance, stupidity, psychological disorder, and a disposition toward violence that might well turn genocidal. And since expressed views help construct the environment in which people are forced to live, any expression of such views is itself considered a form of violence that must, one way or another, be suppressed.

## Bigoted inclusiveness

More generally, any expectation that people will abide by the traditional norms of a particular society, any effort to protect those norms, any failure to treat the private or cultural norms of others as equal in all settings, is considered hateful and abusive. If you say, for example, that Italians and Pashtuns differ, and in Rome one should do more as the Romans do, or that British, American, or Western people have their own identity and interests that deserve the protection of their governments, you are called a white supremacist who deserves to be crushed. After all, is not a

---

[1] See discussion of United States v. Windsor below.

## The Aggressiveness of the Attack

Pashtun migrant, who made a positive choice for Italy and (presumably) dreams only of making a new and better life there, an Italian and indeed more Italian than the Italians? If he follows his own culture, is he not enriching Italy by expanding the definition of what it is to be Italian? Rome herself once grew and became great by incorporating new citizens. As one of her great dramatists said, *homo sum: humani nihil a me alienum puto*—"I am a man: I consider nothing human alien."

Or so people say, and the very oddity of such views increases their ferocity. Abolishing reality cannot be done by halves. Proponents recognize on some level that a shared system of stable identities similar to the inherited one is basic to human life. But that inarticulate recognition increases their fanaticism, because it makes them feel the shakiness of the new moral order on which they insist. The result is rarely second thoughts,[2] but rather intensified efforts to uproot all sense of settled identity and its possible functions, and repeated moral panics about the "bigots" and "haters" supposedly lurking everywhere who refuse to get with the program.

To fight such attitudes and reverse their presumed effects, new rights amounting to a new system of privilege have been established. After all, all identities and lifestyles are equally worthy, at least if they are tolerant of others and do not directly interfere with the government or economy, and each must be presumed equally valuable in every setting. So why allow any inequality to be associated with them? The result is that inclusion—equal presence and success for all groups in all settings—becomes a basic moral necessity. If there are too few black female mathematicians, then standards and selection procedures must change to rectify the injustice. If the remedy involves what looks like special treatment, or changes in standards that seem functionally important, that is simply an illusion created by our society's normalization of the systemic bigotry that accepts certain qualities as more common in some groups than others.

Hardly any respectable person or organization is willing to contest such views publicly. We are deluged with propaganda

---

2 But see George Packer, "When the Culture War Comes for the Kids."

about the oppressiveness of the old system and the glories of the new. The old socially supported roles of wife and mother were inhumanly oppressive, or so it is said, but it is liberating for single mothers to work low-paid clerical or service jobs and raise gender-questioning children with the aid of electronic entertainment and government-provided social services. Similarly, white Christian middle-class standards oppressed the poor and minorities, and were simply a device for maintaining illegitimate power. For minorities to accept such standards is to internalize oppression. So drugs, crime, hip-hop culture, and unwed motherhood must be celebrated, obfuscated, or blamed on discrimination. No one mentions that black economic progress, which had been rapid in the preceding decades, stalled, and black crime rates and thus black victimization by criminals went through the roof,[3] after the triumph of the Civil Rights Movement and social liberalism generally.

To back the propaganda and deal with the supposed threat to human decency posed by skepticism about the new order or by residual attachment to Western systems of identity, our governing classes and their hangers-on supplement formal sanctions on "hate speech," "harassment," and the like with informal ones like shaming, ostracism, loss of employment, and social media lynch mobs. The penalties become ever more severe and are applied ever more widely, since all offenses against the established order are lumped together. So it is thought that someone who opposes COVID-19 restrictions or doubts the legitimacy of an election won by a Democrat is a Nazi, or at least a white supremacist, and should be treated as such—that is, as someone with no rights of any kind that need be respected.[4]

The stated intention of all this "inclusiveness" is the promotion

---

[3] Shaylyn Romney Garrett and Robert D. Putnam, "Why Did Racial Progress Stall in America?"

[4] Consider the treatment of the January 6 demonstrators pursued by the Department of Justice. See Julie Kelly and Lee Smith, *January 6: How Democrats Used the Capitol Protest to Launch a War on Terror against the Political Right*. Also consider the attempt by GoFundMe to divert to its own purposes funds contributed to support demonstrating Canadian truckers.

of unity. In fact it has provoked Brexit and the Trump phenomenon, with their contrary emphasis on the decisive importance of at least national identity, and is now provoking a fundamental rejection of national institutions by much of the population. Proponents of "inclusiveness" have responded by describing Brexit and Trump supporters, often bluntly, as irrational, bigoted, racist, xenophobic, fascist, willfully stupid, and so on. And they found Joe Biden's inaugural address, which implied that his opponents are liars, white supremacists, and domestic terrorists, "unifying." The current war against "bigotry" has thus led not to unity but to the increasing alienation of half the population and a tendency among influential people to treat that half as outside the bounds of legitimate civic participation.

# Examples

The justices of the United States Supreme Court have rarely been stupid, uninformed, unadvised, irrational, or incapable of adjusting their positions to complex considerations. They spend years working closely together and know each other well. The way they are appointed and confirmed generally ensures they are reasonable, "mainstream" people. And several recent justices have been conservative Catholics able to argue intelligently for the natural and traditional definition of marriage. Even so, the majority in United States v. Windsor, a 2013 estate tax decision, found that a statute that did not recognize homosexual unions as marriages "is invalid, for no legitimate purpose overcomes the purpose and effect to disparage and to injure those whom the State, by its marriage laws, sought to protect in personhood and dignity."[5] So there is no reason to recognize a distinction between the sexes with regard to sexual unions. People who favor the natural, traditional, functional, and until very recently universal definition of marriage as a fundamental social institution that precedes the state and thus the Supreme Court itself simply want to disparage and injure others. And this principle is enshrined in the fundamental law of the United States.

---

5  United States v. Windsor, 25–26 (slip opinion).

Among many other examples in the Church, we have Fr Antonio Spadaro, the editor of *La Civiltà Cattolica* and one of the pope's close associates, defining political opposition to abortion and same-sex marriage among American Catholics and Evangelicals as a bizarre "ecumenism of conflict that unites them in the nostalgic dream of a theocratic type of state."[6] The essay in which those words appeared was remembered and thought worthy of recommendation by the pope himself more than two years after its publication.[7] So if you think natural law applies to present-day societies, so that marriage is marriage, an unborn child is an unborn child, and we should all act accordingly, you are a hater abusing religion to impose your arbitrary will. That view is now presented as self-evident in the highest levels of the Church.[8]

---

[6] Antonio Spadaro and Marcelo Figueroa, "Evangelical Fundamentalism and Catholic Integralism in the USA: A Surprising Ecumenism."

[7] Antonio Spadaro, "The Pontiff Meets the Jesuits of Mozambique and Madagascar."

[8] For another example of views on identity among today's prestigious Christian thinkers, including Catholics, see the "Open Letter Against the New Nationalism" published in *Commonweal in* August 2019. It appears from the letter that any attachment to nation that goes beyond attachment to a particular legal regime is incipiently Nazi.

# 5

# Intellectual Background

Most people are stubbornly attached to traditional identities, the universal features of which make it clear they reflect something basic in human life. People in positions of influence should—at a minimum—take seriously the consequences of trying to disrupt and suppress them. The less they understand about how they work, the more cautious they should be. Why then do so many claim, without argument or analysis, that traditional identities, and implicitly the traditional arrangements to which they relate—family, religion, particular community, along with the standards and distinctions that support them—are ungrounded, atavistic, and illegitimate? Why do they regard people attached to them with fear, hatred, and contempt, and project such attitudes onto the objects of their loathing? And why do they insist that chosen identities with no objective basis or social function deserve absolute deference?

## Ruling class madness

The views admissible in public discussion are always determined by the consensus of influential people on fundamental issues. Normally, such hierarchies of influence are beneficial and even socially necessary. They focus discussion so it can make progress, and ensure that the thought of qualified people influences popular belief, correcting it and making it more solid, coherent, and reasonable. After all, if people who hold positions of influence do not know what makes sense with regard to matters for which their position makes them responsible, who will?

A major purpose of education is to organize and strengthen this function. It trains us to accept what those believe who are in a position to know better. Today, though, it is evident that what qualified people say often makes very little sense. So why have well-connected, highly functional, and in many ways well-informed people in a very successful society like our own come to insist on views that are so radically at odds with reality? In other words, why has public reason gone mad? One answer is that success overreaches, pride goes before destruction, and wisdom comes only through suffering. A stable and prosperous society that suppresses risk and makes consumer satisfaction a supreme standard does away with reality checks and becomes susceptible to groundless fantasy and wishful thinking. If such a society claims to be founded on reason, it corrupts reason to support its favored delusions. The more successful the society, the longer it can do so before practical considerations force change.

## Industrialized thought

A more specific answer is that intellectual life has become institutional, blinkered, and uniform because the reconfiguration of social relations on commercial, bureaucratic, and technological lines has led to the industrialization of thought: mass higher education, extreme specialization, and insistence on credentials. The growth of electronic communications, which bathe us in catchy but misleading messages and dissolve reality into myriad images and sound bites that can be reassembled to mean anything whatever, has also played a role.[1] These trends work together to destroy common sense, swamp or suppress free intellectual life, divert attention from everyday experience, channel talented people into narrow bureaucratic or scholarly careers in which they rise by doing what pleases superiors and funding agencies, and create an intellectual mass mind.[2] The result is that supposedly informed opinion increasingly reflects not reality but institu-

---

1 Jacques Ellul notes that the indigestible mass of information in which modern education and journalism buries us is what makes the great success of modern propaganda possible. See his *Propaganda: The Formation of Men's Attitudes*. The development of electronic communications has only made things worse.

2 See Johan S.G. Chu and James A. Evans, "Slowed Canonical Progress in Large Fields of Science." The more scientists and publications there are, the slower fundamental progress becomes.

tional bias. People fail upwards in American public life today. If someone supports the things that conform to institutional commitments—transgenderism, constant foreign intervention, mass immigration, "closing the gap" in group achievement—then the mere fact that his proposals fail and predictions turn out false will not injure his career. His resolute adherence to what is thought to be good and true in spite of all evidence will count as proof of his soundness. He will never say anything that challenges the commitments of the institutions now dominant, so people who run things will treat him as serious and reliable. He will help them maintain the apparent accuracy of their vision of the world and thus the soundness of their claim to rule. That is why someone like Donald Trump, a man who has never had a boss, has always done what he pleased, has no known intellectual interests, and to all appearances is ineducable, retains a better grasp on reality than those who seem his intellectual betters. That is one big reason he was rejected by our entire ruling class the way the body rejects an incompatible skin graft.

## Technocratic ideals

Granted that institutional developments have flattened and narrowed public thought and discussion, and disconnected them from reality, why do they reflect the particular assumptions and conclusions they do?

A basic reason is that institutions and the people who run them have adopted a technological ideal that tells them that rational action consists precisely in the efficient, orderly, and technically rational use of available resources for whatever goals happen to be chosen. This ideal turns traditional and philosophical patterns of the good life into a matter of private taste. The religious, community, and cultural traditions and institutions that embodied these patterns can no longer be viewed as basic to the social order, but only as optional pursuits that should not be allowed to affect those who do not choose them. The result is a technocratic society ordered by global markets and transnational bureaucracies that is hostile to traditional religion, culture, identities, and ways of life.

Proponents view our emerging public order, which in its earlier stages was brought about less by progressive theorists and radicals in power than by practical responses to events such as war, with its demand for social unity, central control, and increased efficiency and production, and by reformist strategies widely thought to represent justice and reason, as moderate, reasonable, non-dogmatic, and non-utopian. Next to some modern regimes, Marxist-Leninist ones for example, most Western governments today are no doubt moderate and reasonable. Even so, the abstract simplicity of the ultimate principles of liberal technocracy gives it a dogmatic and utopian character that grows stronger as its logic works itself out.

That logic excludes from the public sphere considerations as basic to human life as the distinction between the sexes, the need for particular settled community, and the aspiration toward transcendence. The result has been a horrific mismatch between reality and belief, between what people are and what they are thought to be, and consequently a chasm between aspiration and achievement. For example, the radical form of human autonomy now promoted provides very little actual autonomy. It is an autonomy that uproots and isolates people, depriving them of any settled self-understanding or plan of life that connects them to a moral community. The result is that they lose a social setting in which they can attain basic human goals such as stable family life and community connection and respect, and the way is cleared for the power of money and bureaucracy to grow without limit.

The blinkered outlook and narcissism of those who run the system blind them to such problems. They consider their views entirely reasonable, and believe that it is people dragging their feet on innovations such as transgenderism and the effective abolition of national borders who have gone crazy and become enemies of freedom, reason, and the flourishing of human identity.

## Metaphysical confusion

The dominance of technocratic ideals has many causes. A fundamental one is an understanding of reason and reality that makes technocracy seem rationally inevitable, and so makes it difficult for educated and well-placed people to oppose it. This under-

## Intellectual Background

standing eliminates the conception of knowledge as contemplation of ultimate realities that include the goods that properly guide action. It divides the world into the mechanically predictable and therefore knowable realm of modern physics, which is considered the real world, and the free but rationally inscrutable realm of subjectivity. The latter, in spite of what is thought its doubtful ultimate reality, is the source of all evaluation and thus of politics and morality. Our freedom to evaluate the world as we wish and effectuate our choices through technology is thought to make us the world's lawmakers, and that is considered the basis of our human dignity. The choices we make manifest that dignity, and since they are all equally choices they are thought to have equal dignity and an equal claim to fulfillment, subject to the efficiency, reliability, and coherence of the system as a whole.

That understanding of knowledge, reality, and morality naturally leads to the liberal technocratic outlook, which combines the modern scientific emphasis on control of the world around us with the demand that the control be used to realize the goals each of us chooses, as much and equally as possible. The two sides of the outlook support each other: technology facilitates preference satisfaction, while an emphasis on preference satisfaction demands improvements in technology. But such an outlook is radically at odds with traditional concepts of identity, which have little to do with technology or physical science, and place us in a system we did not create that is oriented toward goods we did not choose and tell us that our position in the system defines who we are. Instead, it makes each of us a little deity whose wishes create what we are and the moral reality we inhabit, and makes vindication of our equal divinity, through defense of our equal right to choose, the goal of political and moral life. Hence the religious quality of causes like inclusiveness, multiculturalism, and abortion: they are required by respect for our equal divinity, so rejecting them is a sort of blasphemy.

And that blasphemy is thought especially dangerous because our individual divinity is always in jeopardy. The understanding of reality as technological aligns with the outlook of people with power, so the vision of each individual as divine tends to slide back socially into a view of him as an object among other objects, to be used by other people for their own purposes. And since we are socially constructed as well as divine, social failure to validate our divinity dissolves it: a man will find it much more difficult to see himself as a woman if other people do not acknowledge himself as such. The resulting threat to the moral order and our fundamental dignity as human beings whose choices are respected leads to the hysterical fears visible in the constant talk of "safety." People really do feel the failure of others to cater to their self-understanding as something very much like encroaching annihilation.

## Shrunken horizons

But why understand knowledge, reason, and reality in the narrow way present-day public thought demands? Why not recognize that we have a variety of goods, there are particular things that make us who we are, our capacity for understanding the world and acting intelligently has a variety of sources and purposes, and the world is what it is without regard to us? Institutional interests explain some of the attraction of the present view, but the absolute certainty attached to it seems strange when there are evident alternatives that are more adequate to our experience of life.

Medieval thinkers tended to view our knowledge of the world in a commonsensical Aristotelian way. A tree as we experience it is the real tree, so knowledge that orders and sums up our reflective experience of the tree is knowledge of the tree as it really is. In particular, the tree is a unity of form and matter, and thus an instance of a specific kind of thing with a specific natural identity, that comes into being through the doings of things other than itself, acts in ways that bring about certain states of affairs such as growth and reproduction, and so on.

That is still a natural way for people to understand the world, and when dealing with living things it is a practical necessity. An apple tree has a complex of features that makes it the kind of thing it is, as well as natural tendencies that conditions can favor or not. If you do not keep those things in mind you will not have much success managing an orchard. But that way of looking at things is now considered a sort of stopgap that intellectually upright people try to avoid when possible. If they want to feel intellectually respectable when they talk about trees, they would rather talk about molecular biology than characteristic forms, patterns, and ways of acting. The former seems rigorous, the latter subjective and impressionistic. So they talk about the mechanisms of life rather than life itself.[3]

Characteristic forms and patterns also drop out of other discussions that aspire to respectability. With regard to politics, for example, most people today would rather be guided by statistics, legal arrangements, organizational charts, market fluctuations, simple relations of cause and effect, and abstract principles like equality than innate patterns of behavior and the ways particular traditions reflect them. The latter may be more useful, but they are difficult to define with mathematical precision, and less adapted to the design of social policy. Worse, they are politically suspect. What, someone might ask, are these characteristic patterns that are supposedly so important? Families? Inherited behavioral tendencies? The sexual binary? Historically evolved communities? It would be racist, sexist, and heteronormative to take such things seriously and accept that human beings have innate features and ways of acting, including attachment to particular cultural communities, that are basic to how they live. The practical conclusion is that it is better—certainly, more convenient—to ignore such things, lie about them, or abolish them in thought by denying them any stable definition.

## Scientism

This radically anti-traditional approach toward knowledge, often called "scientism," goes back to the rise of modern natural science. Francis Bacon was a leading figure in that development. He wanted us to "put nature to the question"—that is, perform experiments—so we could derive knowledge useful for the "relief of man's estate." The intended result was to make exact measurement, prediction, and control central to the study of nature. That meant treating the physical world as much as possi-

---

[3] See the articles collected at Stephen L. Talbott, "Recovering the Organism."

ble as a collection of objects with purely numerical attributes such as size, shape, and mass acting in accordance with mathematical laws.

So instead of contemplation—concern with truth simply as such—the new science that grew up in the seventeenth century would promote technology. Instead of explanations of general features of the world we see around us that help us understand it as a system we take part in, researchers would seek exact numerical knowledge that enables us to control it. Galileo, who emphasized measurement, and Descartes, who thought the physical world was purely mathematical in character, pioneered that approach. A major point was rejection of essences and teleology. In Aristotelian language, moderns decided to ignore formal and final cause—explanations involving characteristic structures and the states of affairs toward which they tend. They did not want to look at a man and explain health by reference to overall bodily structure and functioning and what might restore the ability to maintain the body in its best state. Instead, they wanted to look at detailed mechanisms. That approach, they believed, was more concrete, and more likely to enable us to devise interventions that help us achieve whatever our goals might be.

This approach has been enormously successful on its own terms. Modern natural science and the medical technology based on it cure disease more effectively than Galen ever did. The modern approach has therefore replaced the traditional one, which was based on long experience with natural systems such as the body and how to work with them. Its successes, not only in medicine but in many other practical arts, seem to support its unique validity. Technological thought has therefore become more and more pervasive, and in public settings all but universal and absolute. Educated people today who have an explicit view on the matter generally believe that the real world is simply the world described by modern physics and technology. Such views are basic to the global economic and political order now emerging, in part because of their effectiveness but also in part because they are more readily available to all participants than other general views, such as Confucianism or the Western natural law tradition. Reason must be common to all, and the only thought all accept today is technological, so technology is now treated as if it exhausted reason.

We have thus come to live intellectually in a sort of truncated Cartesian world in which the purely mathematical objects and relationships studied by modern physics are considered the ultimate constituents of reality. Descartes thought these mathematical objects had to be supplemented by non-physical realities such as mind to account for the world as we find it. People today are trying, not very successfully, to do without the latter, and understand the world as purely material.

The success of a method of investigating certain questions does not mean that it will succeed everywhere, let alone give us the ultimate truth about reality. And the commonly accepted story of modern natural science is in fact oversimplified. Scientism does not really account for what scientists do, since they need insight into how physical systems work, which involves formal and final causes—i.e., how systems are laid out and how they function.[4] Philosophers of science have tried to deal with that issue by distinguishing the context of discovery, which brings in all aspects of how scientists actually think about their subject matter, from the context of justification, in which narrower and more rigorous ways of thinking apply. The distinction may be useful to philosophers, but it undercuts the popular view that modern natural science gives a clear, simple, and comprehensive account of what the world is really like.

Public discussion ignores such complications. Metaphysics is difficult and uncertain, so why not go with what looks simplest, and stick with well-defined physical objects and their mechanical interactions as our total account of reality—especially when doing so is consistent with established political, social, and moral commitments? People like explanations that simplify things even when they leave out obvious truths, because they make complex realities seem manageable. That is especially true of people who want to run a world that is far too complicated to understand.

---

[4] For a discussion of the unrecognized relevance of Aristotle's thought to the solution of difficulties within modern science itself, see Benjamin Liebeskind, "Einstein in Athens."

And those carrying on an inquiry succeed by exaggerating the value and importance of what they do, and when they have successes other people are impressed and accept their self-assessment. That is what has happened with modern natural science.

## Subjectivism

So educated people now believe that the real world is numerical and mechanical. But if so, what happens to our experience, which has features like sensation that are neither? After all, the subjective quality of our sensation of redness is not something that can be fully captured by numbers. Since modern physical science cannot deal with such matters, when it is accepted as the model for all knowledge experience becomes unknowable—a paradox.

As a rational matter, modern natural science would support Cartesian dualism, at least as a strategy for understanding the world around us: there is body, which natural science studies, and there are other realities such as mind, which must be studied some other way. But the connection between the two has been difficult to make sense of, and people who want a clear system of general principles have responded by rejecting mind as an objective reality and viewing it as subjective or illusory—whatever sense it makes to say mind is an illusion. The Cartesian revolution, which started with individual consciousness as the basis for all knowledge, has ended by denying that individual consciousness is real. But the attempt to get rid of something as basic as consciousness only brings it back in lawless form. The scientistic view means that the world is no longer seen as an integrated system in which nature, whether the human body or the cosmos, can have meaning and moral implications. There are space, time, matter, and energy, which are purely mathematical and can mean nothing apart from whatever meaning we arbitrarily project onto them, and there is subjectivity—sensation, feeling, thought, desire, and will. The latter has no intelligible connection to anything outside itself, so it is thrown back on itself to decide what things mean.

Meaning thus becomes something we make up. And since beliefs depend on meanings, the same eventually applies to our entire understanding of the world. The only world we can know is the world of our own mental constructions. The attempt to make modern natural science the model for all knowledge, which started as an attempt at total objectivity, thus ends in total subjectivity, since it cannot account for knowledge itself and so consigns it in principle to a world of free-floating fantasy. However the resultant subjectivism may conflict with technocratic ways of thinking, both flow from the original decision to exclude form and finality from our understanding of reality, thus destroying the objectivity of goods and meanings.

The United States Supreme Court has repeatedly treated subjectivist principles as basic to the fundamental law of the United States. In the famous "mystery passage" of Planned Parenthood v. Casey, the court tells us that "at the heart of liberty is the right to define one's own concept of existence, of meaning, of the universe, and of the mystery of human life." Since liberty is thought to define the United States as a political society, it follows that our fundamental principle as a society is that everyone establishes his own cosmic and moral reality, and everyone else must accept that reality as valid. So if a man says he is a woman he is a woman, if a mother does not think her unborn child is a child she can dispose of it as she wishes, and if a same-sex couple thinks their relationship is a marriage then everyone must accept it as such. Such views are considered irrefutable: truth is now a construction, evidence becomes evidence only if we treat it as such, and identity—what something is—is entirely a human decision.

As a statement of theoretical commitments generally accepted by educated and well-placed people, the court's statement in *Casey* is correct. That is why traditional natural law no longer makes sense to such people, and they are so outraged by any judicial refusal to treat their commitments as plain reality. Morality, politics, and identity, all respectable authority tells them, can have nothing to do with natural goals, classifications, and ways of functioning, because the latter do not exist. The results are vividly on display in current attitudes toward sex, which is assumed to have no intrinsic nature or meaning and so becomes a pure matter of individual choice with no defined function. In the coming years we will see the full effect of this increasing subjectivism.

The technocratic aspects of our public thought have proven enormously effective in building modern industry, modern technology, and the modern state. How far our rulers will be able to maintain the coherence and efficiency of the system in the face of rising subjectivist tendencies is uncertain.

# 6
# Practical Background

How did so many people come to adopt this narrow but powerful understanding of knowledge, rationality, and reality? Why the switch in standards from contemplation and the good to desire and control? The ancients and medievals often sought control so they could get what they wanted, but apart from the sophists their men of thought and learning did not propose those things as the highest goods.

## Historical

There are several ways to tell the story. Scholars trace the rise of scientism back to earlier intellectual tendencies, but for this discussion it seems more illuminating to refer to social developments. A common account is that people in the early modern period got tired of disputes that could not be settled. Scholastic philosophy was not going anywhere, and disputes over religion had led to bloody religious wars. So they decided to stick to things that were practical and demonstrable, or at least could be agreed on by as many people as possible. Hence the rise of modern natural science based on repeatable, quantifiable observations, and of a utilitarian and technological approach to social questions. Both worked, so people stuck with them, and modernity was truly launched.

This story glorifies the present by falsifying the past. Early modernity brought not only the rise of modern natural science but a greater interest in magic, an alternative way to dominate man and nature, that was represented not only by the witch craze that affected all levels of society but by the interest in alchemy, astrology, Hermeticism, and Kabbalah among the intellectual elite. As modernity developed, it brought illiberalism—

fascism and communism—as well as liberalism, and is increasingly pushing liberalism itself toward rejection of free and rational thought. And it has brought wars and massacres on an unprecedented scale, carried out for reasons that are far less rational than those that guided princes during the Wars of Religion. So the modern period has involved much more than technological advances and universal ideals.

In any event, the so-called Wars of Religion were not simply or perhaps even primarily religious. Princes wanted to increase their wealth and power by consolidating state power and increasing their resources. That effort often meant war, and it had nothing to do with confessional oppositions. So it is not surprising that the most destructive phases of the Thirty Years War pitted Catholic France and Lutheran Sweden against the Catholic Empire, and the Peace of Westphalia that ended it brought the principle of state supremacy over religion: *cuius regio eius religio*. In the end, the Wars of Religion thus turned out to be wars for the increase of state power through state control of religion. Princes appealed to religion to motivate their supporters, but for the most part secular political considerations were more important.

Such considerations were what made the Protestant revolt possible. To increase their power, princes wanted to take control of the Church and her property, whether by limiting Roman influence or by breaking from Rome altogether. Religious dissidents who would previously have gotten nowhere, or accepted that they had to work more or less within the established system of religion, therefore found a ready audience for extreme measures. And those princes who remained Catholic found ways to strengthen their position with respect to a Church that was now in no position to resist them. From this perspective modern directions in thought, religion, and politics have had less to do with a sense that contemplative philosophy and Christendom had proved themselves pointless, self-defeating, or dangerous than with the desire for power. In the words of Thomas Hobbes, they have had to do with "a perpetual and restless desire of power after power, that ceaseth only in death."[1] Their most fit-

---

[1] Thomas Hobbes, *Leviathan*, 65.

ting symbols are not universal suffrage and the Republic of Letters but barracks and arms factories.

## Economic

The desire for power has always been with us, but the development of technology made it easier to satisfy, and eventually enabled it to achieve full practical and intellectual dominance in the form of technological society. While liberalism and technocracy speak of freedom, equality, and reason, they turn them into principles of rule and thus of power and hierarchy. In that development political and intellectual tendencies, economic and institutional changes, and the needs of power have all cooperated.

## Industrial society

These tendencies have led to today's industrial society, in which major social functions like government, education, manufacturing, and the provision of most services are carried on through large impersonal organizations backed by large capital investments in up-to-date technology, and coordinated through bureaucratic expertise and geographically extensive markets. People have been complaining about that form of society since it began, but cannot seem to do without it because it is so effective. If we got rid of it we would all starve, die in the next pandemic, or get conquered by a country that retained such a system. Or so it seems—there are those who point out advantages in more traditional approaches, for example with regard to agriculture, building, and urban design, but so far their views have not caught on.

From the beginning novelists exposed industrialization's seamy side. Artists and designers complained about its effect on popular taste. Poets who lived like beatniks dreamed of more romantic ages in which people lived like villagers, aristocrats, saints, and kings. Adam Smith and then Karl Marx admired its productivity, but had concerns. Smith doubted the public spirit of those who ran it and worried about its stupefying effect on workers.[2] Marx

---

[2] See *An Inquiry into the Nature and Causes of the Wealth of Nations*, chapter X, part II, and Nathan Rosenberg, "Adam Smith on the Division of Labour: Two Views or One?"

hated it, and predicted people would eventually get fed up and get rid of it. The Revolution, he claimed, would establish a utopia of freedom and plenty, but when it arrived it brought an incomparably more brutal and oppressive form of the same thing. And popes, ordinary Catholics, and reformers of all kinds proposed ways to transform it or at least alleviate the problems it created.

But what were those problems? People who take an economic view of things talk about poverty and the exploitation of workers. And it is true that industrialization extended working hours, concentrated poverty in urban slums, exposed workers to the vagaries of the business cycle, cut personal ties between them and their employers, and produced great fortunes that made severe poverty seem more shocking. But was poverty less common or less severe before industrialization? It seems not, given the rise in population that followed it. And since industrialization increases production, and forces employers to compete for workers, it seems that the more industry grows the higher wages should go. And that is the way things have turned out. Even today, stagnating wages in developed countries are more than offset by rising prosperity elsewhere, fueled by world trade.

So poverty is not the problem. Inequality is more of an issue, since industrialization increases differences in economic productivity, and wealth sticks to those who are well-placed in large networks and organizations. But inequalities are always with us, and they do not make a decent life impossible.

## A mechanical world

The real problem with industrialism is the one Emerson noted: "things are in the saddle and ride mankind." Large systems that integrate complex machinery, the latest technology, and rigorously formalized procedures are extremely effective at realizing concrete goals—producing food, clothing, and shelter, traveling to the moon, or destroying the enemy in war. But they have deficiencies. A traditional art or craft accepts the nature of its materials, with their special quirks. So traditional husbandry, medicine, and cooking took various features and tendencies of living forms as given and worked with them. Agribusiness, Big Pharma, and the food industry take a very different approach. They break down objects and situations into their simplest components and develop set routines that work equally well everywhere to achieve whatever goal is specified. But the human element gets lost. Workers lose individuality, choice, and craftsmanship, and what is produced loses the human touch. If someone makes shoes, he is no longer making the best shoe he can for a particular customer he knows personally, using his skill to fit the customer's taste, foot, and pocketbook. Instead, he is tending a machine that repeatedly performs one part of the process of producing a shoe. And the shoe will not be for anyone in particular. Instead, it will be designed for the average foot, and made no better than needed for maximum profit.

The result of this transformation of the nature of work is that shoes and other goods become worse, but also much cheaper. The change may be worth it when survival is at stake. Famines are horrible, and industrial agriculture, with machinery, chemical fertilizer, insecticides, and hybrid seeds, produces a great deal of food. It may not be as good, and the change may cause other problems, but it is far more plentiful. India, which had been subject to famine, increased annual wheat production from 10 million tons in the 1960s to 73 million in 2006 by making farming more industrial.[3] And industrial medicine, with anesthesia, antibiotics, vaccines, and an ever-growing array of technological interventions into the human body, saves countless lives.

So it is hard to turn down the benefits of industrialization. Even so, it is dehumanizing and to all appearances cannot stop being so. As such, it has greatly contributed to abolishing the social influence of human nature, history, culture, and religion, and thus to abolishing traditional systems of identity. After all, what do faith, family life, ancestral heritage, or the distinction between man and woman have to do with a computer network, financial system, oil refinery, or code of government regulations? And if the latter are the things we live by, why not get rid of irrelevancies that just get in the way? In fact, why not turn the whole world into a big industrial process? And that is what current ten-

---

[3] Torsten Kurth et al., "Reviving Agricultural Innovation in Seeds and Crop Protection."

dencies are doing. The industrial order wants to turn everything it deals with into a mass of graded resources differentiated only by criteria relevant to a technological process of production. That tendency applies to human resources as much as to petroleum and ball bearings. And interchangeable people do not have stable and functional personal identities any more than interchangeable machine parts do.

### Tyranny as liberation

Political and ideological trends thus reflect the development of industrial society. Technical improvements enable the wealthy and powerful to bring about social and political changes that advance their self-interested goals but are considered progressive because they further the process of social rationalization. For example, trade and managerial bureaucracy oppose national boundaries because they limit the scope of their activity and establish settings in which traditional institutions and understandings that restrain them can maintain authority. Similarly, they are adverse to traditional marriage and sex roles because they create stubborn ties that complicate social control—disputes between parents and school boards are a recent example—and the use of men and women as interchangeable, always-available resources for the economic system. Improved communications and transportation facilitate a borderless world, and factories, power machinery, the service economy, the mechanization of housework, and the socialization of child-rearing make it possible to put women in the same workforce as men; they also radically reduce the practical importance of family ties and the traditional understandings of identity associated with them.

"Social progress" as now defined thus goes hand in hand with the development of technology and the growth of centralized wealth and power. A just and rational society—in theory, one that gets everyone what he wants, as much and as equally, reliably, and efficiently as possible—is now understood as a sort of European Union writ large, a system based on world markets combined with transnational bureaucracies run by experts on economics, social welfare, business administration, and human rights. Such a system is considered uniquely legitimate because uniquely fitted to promote peace, prosperity, and justice. What it actually does is merge capitalism and progressivism into a single system of power run by a partnership of billionaires and bureaucrats. Other more traditional principles of order, such as family, religion, and nationality, involve connections and differentiations that have no obvious basis in efficiency or technological rationality, and are therefore viewed as pointless burdens on society. All power and social functioning must, for ostensibly high-minded reasons, be placed in the hands of commercial and bureaucratic interests. Even mutual support and cooperation within the family are disfavored, since it is impossible to regulate and equalize the conditions, division, and rewards of "unpaid housework." Apparently, something that is not part of a commercial or bureaucratic structure can be legitimate only as a strictly personal pursuit serving one's own interests and desires.

With all this in mind, it is not surprising that the collapse of communism and consequent triumph of liberal politics and economics was immediately followed by the rise of "gay marriage" as a serious political issue. With its only serious competitor gone, our system was free to develop in accordance with its own inner tendencies without regard to the opinions of ordinary people or effect on social solidarity. And "gay marriage" is important for the system as a matter of principle: it completes the destruction of marriage and the family as fundamental natural institutions with an intrinsic function and structure that connects the social order to man's body, soul, past, and future.

More generally, settled identities and understandings of human nature limit our rulers' ability to reconfigure man and society, and suggest that there are standards for what is good independent of money and bureaucracy. Why should the powerful want that? They would rather be able to transform reality any way they want. Particular actors of course have their own motives. A bureaucrat might be motivated by personal ambition, self-interest, envy, or animosity, by a fondness for petty tyranny, or by genuine concern for the poor. A businessman might want to get cheap praise, divide potential opponents, and distract attention from economic issues by emphasizing diversity and corporate efforts to promote inclusiveness. And the two are likely to be at odds regarding the proper balance of power between business and bureaucracy. But institutional interests and perspectives will lead both to accept a technocratic outlook that eliminates traditional ties and distinctions, as well as to accept the need for an international partnership between business and bureaucracy to run, manage, and continuously reconfigure the social machine without serious interference from the ignorant, short-sighted, and very likely bigoted populace.

Liberalism, the great champion of freedom and equality, thus turns out to be a system made to order for billionaires and bureaucrats that tailors not only its ideals and demands but human beings themselves to their needs. It is leading, for example, to proposals that human beings be fitted with brain implants so that the global economic order can connect to them directly.[4]

But there are limits to the system's promotion of freedom, equality, and fluidity. Equality gives way to the need for incentives and effective management, which in practice means acceptance of enormous inequalities in wealth and power. Idealists may call for subsidiarity and for redistribution of wealth, but the solidity of the partnership between business and bureaucracy, and the growing independence of the resulting structure of governance from popular answerability, make such calls ineffective. Nor can people be allowed actual freedom to pursue any goal they want. Instead, they must be guided toward manageable goals that support the system. So they are encouraged to be politically correct careerists who are otherwise mostly interested in consumer goods, personal indulgences, leisure time activities, and so on. And for the sake of the unperturbed operation of the system, they are required to keep quiet about principles of human connection other than money and bureaucracy. If they do not like the basics of the way things are being run, they should keep it to themselves.

These are the views on which liberalism now insists. Our authoritative cultural and intellectual institutions—universities, charitable foundations, art institutions, religious organizations,

---

4 Raymond Wolfe, "World Economic Forum Head's Prediction of Microchips 'in Our Brains' Is Coming True, Thanks to Big Tech."

big journalism—are monolithically on the side of the anti-traditional social, moral, and political order now establishing global dominance, an order in which multinational corporations and international currency speculators can present themselves as moral leaders in the cause of human autonomy, and in which human nature is considered wholly malleable, so that specific human identities disappear. All the while, the system follows its own laws, which have very little to do with autonomy or other ideal goals. While it claims to liberate the individual, it ends by turning him into a cipher, a generic resource to be managed by business, bureaucracy, and social workers. It speaks of creativity, but reduces everything to one dead level, replacing culture with propaganda, commercial entertainment, and bureaucratically funded "high culture" that no one cares about. Its ideal justification—freedom, equality, inclusiveness, and so on—is thus an ideology in the Marxist sense, a system of principles that justifies rule by those in power and their suppression of competing institutions, authorities, and perspectives.

# PART II
A World Transformed

# 7
# Social Consequences

Liberal insistence that we can define ourselves arbitrarily results in the disintegration of institutions and connections that depend on natural and traditional understandings of identity. But we are social beings, and the disintegration of things that are so natural to us means our disintegration as well. As the social world falls into chaos we lose our reason and humanity.

## End of boundaries

Communities have boundaries; culture exists through particularity; common goods guide action and thus tell people what to do; and settled identities define themselves in part through contrast and thus through opposition. For these reasons community, culture, and settled identity, along with shared conceptions of the common good, are now considered bigoted, oppressive, hateful, and implicitly violent. To achieve liberation, they must all be done away with. But man is a social animal. Abolishing settled ties and relationships disables him, and rejecting the question of the common good makes it impossible for him to pursue the good life in partnership with others. Liberalism thus rejects the aspects of human life in which people find meaning and purpose.

## Human ties dissolve

The insistent secularism of today's progressivism, its rejection of the natural family as a standard, its dissolution of inherited community—in essence, its abolition of God, family, and people as socially recognized realities—express its intrinsic radicalism. The apparent ideal is an aggregate of godless individuals with no settled identities and no family or community connections that matter. Instead of family life, community ties, and transcendent loyalties to order our world, we are to rely on therapy, fast food, day care, pop culture, social services, employee benefits, social media, and consumer choice.

The change is considered liberating, because it abolishes the traditional ties, boundaries, limitations, and authorities that our rulers have declared oppressive. But it is a liberation that alienates people from their past, their surroundings, the people around them, and even—since they no longer know who they are—themselves. We are social beings and not economic abstractions, Nietzschean supermen who create our own moral reality, or machines able to dispense with such concerns. Traditional identities and the social arrangements they articulate—family, religion, cultural community, nation, particular civilization—enable people to understand themselves, connect with others, and think about their lives coherently. Depriving people of such things disrupts all that, and leads to loneliness, depression, feelings of pointlessness, and various addictions and obsessions. Money cannot buy everything, even when supplemented by smartphones, sensitivity training, and a health club membership.

Where secularizers once spoke of liberty, equality, and fraternity they now speak only of liberty and equality, since the destruction of communal bonds and promotion of individualistic and chaotic forms of family life allow fraternity only in the entirely abstract and anti-familial form of inclusiveness. That is bad for everyone.

## Life comes unglued

We have noted the way cultural and civilizational identity brings other aspects of identity, such as sex, family, and religion, into a system that enables us to live a rewarding life with others. Without that, our understanding of who we are becomes idiosyncratic or one-dimensional—I am my career, bank balance, consumer preferences, political opinions, and personal obsessions—and in any case incapable of serving as the basis of a coherent and satisfying way of life.

What, for example, do people do with sex in the Brave New World now upon us? Traditional standards and identities related our physical being, and the physiological and psychological functions and impulses to which it gives rise, to our social being, to the past and future, and even to moral and spiritual realities. That helped us connect inner and outer experience, private life and life in society, immediate impulse and the pattern of our lives with others, and make sense of them all together. Do-it-yourself identities cannot do that, even if they could otherwise succeed in making sense of situations that are complex, subtle, far-reaching, prone to disorder, and dependent on the beliefs and attitudes of others. Whether you are male, female, two-spirit, or pangender is now considered a private construction with no functional significance. But how then can it order anything or connect it to anything else?

The unsettling of something as basic as sexual identity means that sex is a mess, men and women do not know what to do with each other, children—if they are born at all—grow up in a world alien to them and their needs, and marriage is a luxury good for the successful rather than a basic structural feature of social life that gives ordinary men and women a motive for an orderly and productive way of life, along with a secure, respected, and authoritative position in a foundational social institution.

## Institutional wreckage

Family relationships are central to personal identity,[1] but they cannot be talked about reasonably today. They are the foundation of our life with others, but the good life and our relationships with others have been declared a matter of private evaluation and decision, so what is there to say? More practically, talking about such things openly and realistically would bring out the shakiness of certain arrangements common today, and people would see that as a personal attack. To point out problems with unwed motherhood or gay adoption, for example, is now considered an "attack on families."

And certain arrangements common today are indeed shaky. Constant indoctrination into the view that traditional understandings of identity are external impositions, together with

---

[1] See Mary Eberstadt, *Adam and Eve after the Pill: Paradoxes of the Sexual Revolution*.

growing narcissism, individual peculiarities, the disorder of traditional institutions, and the impersonal quality of the social relationships that attempt to replace them have led many people to see traditional understandings as indeed oppressive. They may, for example, speak of themselves as "non-binary," meaning neither male nor female. But what then? Can a satisfactory life really be built on something that is hard to distinguish from fantasy role-playing? Many people say that doing away with the demands imposed by traditional identities improves the lives of those who find them uncomfortable, pointing for example to reports that recognition of "gay marriage" was followed by a reduction in gay suicide. But what happens when the festive feeling wears off, and the difficulty of pulling disorderly and incongruous desires into a sustaining pattern reasserts itself?[2] And what about the far more numerous people who rely in their own lives on a settled functional understanding of masculinity, femininity, and marriage? Turning people into isolated social atoms with no socially supported idea of who they are or what makes sense in their closest relationships is not likely—for example—to make life better for mothers and children. And it hardly seems a sign of happiness to come when surveys suggest that somewhere between 20 and 40 percent of those born between 1997 and 2003 now identify as LGBTQ.[3] The novelty of such developments, together with their faddish aspects[4] and the serious and enduring personal difficulties among those caught up in them,[5] show that they are not a manifestation of permanent human tendencies now beneficially set free by social progress, but rather a result of the disintegration of normal social and psychological order in a society that has turned self-destructive because it no longer supports sane ways of living.

2 Charlotte Björkenstam et al., "Suicide in Married Couples in Sweden: Is the Risk Greater in Same-Sex Couples?"

3 See Jones, "LGBT Identification in U.S. Ticks up to 7.1%" and Paul Bond, "Nearly 40 Percent of U.S. Gen Zs, 30 Percent of Young Christians Identify as LGBTQ, Poll Shows."

4 Shrier, *Irreversible Damage*.

5 Ryan Anderson, "Sex Reassignment Doesn't Work. Here Is the Evidence."

## End of thought

A further consequence of current tendencies, one that makes it very difficult to understand or do anything about our problems, is alienation from reality to a point that might fairly be called insanity.

## Failed meritocracy

We live in something of a meritocracy, and our rulers believe they are the most enlightened and well-informed people who ever lived. That is why they feel entitled, in spite of today's democratic rhetoric, to make their aspirations the standard for all mankind. They are horrified by claims there are principles that transcend those aspirations, viewing such claims as the sort of "fundamentalism" that led to 9/11, and treat the past as worth considering only as something to escape or a foreshadowing of the present. Nonetheless, a variety of conditions, from the state of political discussion to that of education and the arts, makes it evident that Westerners are growing less and less able to think clearly and effectively. Consider, for example, the growing irrationalism of much academic discussion, which emphasizes the feelings and comfort of those involved, views argument as a rhetorical expression of group identity and the will to power, and treats more and more issues as closed. The tendency is infecting even the hard sciences, at least to the extent of affecting rhetoric, funding, and personnel decisions.[6]

## Growing ineffectuality

Technocratic meritocracy leads to stupidity by applying an industrial approach to thought and culture. It centralizes and bureaucratizes them, depriving local efforts of talent and respect and making leaders unable to think or function outside established understandings that reflect institutional interests and prejudices. Those in positions of responsibility mostly went to the same highly competitive schools, where they were all told the same things, and it has taken all their efforts to rise to their positions in

---

[6] Heather Mac Donald, "Woke Science Is an Experiment Certain to Fail."

an extremely competitive hierarchical system. The result is that they are absorbed in their social position, habituated to pleasing their colleagues and superiors, and accustomed to falling entirely in line with institutional perspectives. They would find it very difficult to adopt an independent perspective if the desire to do so ever crossed their minds. It is their position in the system, they believe, that makes them what they are. So what could independence possibly mean to them other than loss of the position it cost them so much to attain?

The results are evident in our public life. Do our public figures and academic experts give the impression that they know what is going on or what to do about it? How often do they say anything that would be of interest if a different name were attached? Can anyone imagine Hilary Clinton saying anything worthwhile?

## Resulting blindness

The bureaucratization of thought means that mistakes never come home to those who commit them, errors are not corrected, thought loses its connection to reality, and irrationality grows ever grosser. Many of the irrationalities have to do with the unwieldiness of expertise as a mass institution—the more experts the less progress can be made, because they get in each other's way[7]—while others have to do with egalitarian demands that require habitual denial of obvious realities. Thus, we have the multiplication of "genders," insistence that different human populations are indistinguishable, open borders as a human right, compulsory celebration of diversity as a universal good, and the public propagation by respected voices of vicious fantasies blaming all the world's problems on sexually normal white Christian men.

Other problems arise because scientism, our official understanding of reality, rejects pattern recognition in favor of mechanical cause and effect, which explain very little in social life. So it has no room for common sense or the concept of the normal, which have to do with recognizing the patterns that order everyday life. In any case, to speak of the normal and of everyday pat-

---

7 Chu and Evans, "Slowed Canonical Progress in Large Fields of Science."

terns is now often considered "hatred." Relating individual cases to patterns of social functioning and making a particular pattern the standard means stereotyping and prejudice, which (we are told) are always irrational and must be eradicated in the name of justice, safety, and liberation from traditional expectations.

This insistent blindness to the world's normal functioning is responsible for much of the mindlessness of current political discussion, the futility of public policy, and the inability of the social sciences to make progress. In education, it means non-stop indoctrination in place of learning, attempts to remodel boys and girls to make them indistinguishable, ever-expanding efforts to transform the culture of science to make it more friendly to women and ethnic minorities, and the elimination of standards in order to eliminate group differences in achievement. Similarly, a major reason for foreign policy failures in the Middle East and Afghanistan has been the stubbornly held view that the people there are just like Americans. All people want freedom, democracy, and consumer satisfactions, or so it is thought, and it would be racist to doubt their ability to secure those goods for themselves once oppressive regimes have been overthrown, progressive NGOs have told them what to do, and free elections have been held. After all, the progressive West is the transparently correct standard to which everything aspires! The results of that belief are visible to all.

## No place for thought

Thought is the attempt to understand the world in an orderly way, and to decide what to do in light both of practicalities and of the good, beautiful, and true. That effort is a normal part of life, but it requires engagement with the world. Propaganda, electronic entertainment, and the distance between cause and effect in a complex globalized society disconnect public understandings from reality. Who can separate truth from distortion when important events are distant and complicated and professionals are paid to obfuscate the issues? Also, functions once performed by individuals, families, and tradition are now carried on by bureaucracy, commerce, and the media. So instead of the arts of life, which require thought, skill, and engagement with immediate concrete circumstances, we have consumer goods, social programs, and industrially produced pop culture, which deaden thought, suppress everyday capabilities, and spread propaganda and fantasy.

Thought also depends on other conditions. It requires a definite point of view, calmness and steadiness of attention, a world that is understood as stable and meaningful, and a willingness to let truth rather than desire or power be the guide. Today these conditions are being destroyed. People are losing a definite point of view, because the destruction of personal identity means they no longer know who they are. As a result they can only look at things from a point of view that is childish, willful, institutional, or constructed for them by pop culture and propaganda. And electronic communications constantly disrupt the steadiness of attention needed to think productively. Marshall McLuhan thought the electronic media would give us a global village. But a village has a structure and way of life that has evolved to work for its members. Instead, the media have given us a global mob constantly in an uproar and a world disintegrated into images and soundbites that can be reassembled to make anything appear true.

Worse, to say that the world is stable and meaningful in some determinable way denies what has become the defining principle of our society: in the Supreme Court's words, "the right to define one's own concept of existence, of meaning, of the universe, and of the mystery of human life."[8] So nothing is settled and every opinion is as valid as every other. But what then is the point of thought?

A further problem is that complex thought requires a tradition of inquiry for issues to develop, insights to accumulate, and both to come into focus and settle into a usable system. We cannot pursue the good, the beautiful, and the true effectively without joining with others who share enough beliefs, memories, and expectations to speak as it were the same language. But today's outlook opposes tradition as a matter of principle. It is always the tradition of a particular community, so it is easily discredited as

---

8 Planned Parenthood of Southeastern Pa. v. Casey.

exclusionary, oppressive, and racist. Thought, it is said, is always situated—it depends on who is doing the thinking. That is no doubt true, since thought is carried on within a tradition, but this does not mean, as is supposed today, that dominant ways of thought simply express the interests and identities of dominant groups and must therefore be rejected as oppressive. And why bother thinking carefully if the results can never have general validity but are simply expressions of one's own identity and social position?

In any event, people today find thought annoying. It sticks up for itself, so it is elitist. It tells people they cannot have what they want. It depends on standards of cogency, which exclude marginalized voices. It requires effort, so it is at odds with comfort, consumerism, and lifestyle libertarianism. And beyond that, nobody influential really wants people to think. Why would they, when that would make life complicated for people who run things? They want useful workers, compliant citizens, consumers who make harmless choices, and "critical thinkers," who in fact are those who reject tradition and common sense in favor of whatever official experts tell them.

# 8

# Human Realities

Liberalism promises freedom, equality, and unconditional respect. But the attempt to realize those things through a comprehensive rational system of control destroys them, along with the stable systems of identity and relationship needed for a tolerable way of life, because it destroys human connection, agency, and identity. The result is individual isolation, social fragmentation, servitude to billionaires and bureaucrats, and denial that anything about us matters except the qualities our rulers want to make use of.

## Daily life

For generations, the technocratic ideal has been sweeping all before it. Everything must be made equal, efficient, and rational. So all aspects of life—work, education, entertainment, and daily practicalities like cooking and the care of the young, sick, aged, and unfortunate—are now dealt with through commercial and bureaucratic institutions rather than the familial, religious, and communal arrangements once customary.

The tendency toward overall industrial organization is strengthened by its effectiveness in many respects, as well as factors like ease of travel, increase in demographic diversity, and all-pervasive electronic communications. These factors weaken concrete connections and make people, places, and things more easily and rapidly present to each other. This seems to make comprehensive rational organization possible, and helps motivate our current attempt to take care of all needs and desires through a combination of individual decision and the industrial, bureaucratic, and market processes through which these decisions can be aggregated, reconciled, and carried out. Nature, history, tradition, and traditional identities become irrelevant.

Under such circumstances, what hiding place is there for anything at odds with dominant institutions and understandings? Amusements, practical needs, and even what people eat for breakfast are provided by global markets and huge bureaucratic organizations. Career success and the fulfillments allowed by the system—participating in it and enjoying the consumer goods and lifestyle freedoms it affords—seem to be the sole goals life offers. What else is there, when traditional arrangements have been weakened and suppressed, and so have difficulty maintaining coherence and functionality, and we are bathed in attacks on the traditional identities that link us to them?

## A new morality

This situation has profound moral consequences. Legitimate distinctions among human beings are reduced to those necessary for the system: wealth, bureaucratic position, social and political orthodoxy, and skills and training relevant to employment. With regard to other distinctions, diversity, equality, and inclusion become sacred principles. Lifestyle and our relationships with others must therefore become wholly a matter of individual choice. Traditional boundaries must be abolished as pointlessly oppressive: every historical and cultural community, with its particular standards, authorities, boundaries, and understandings of identity, must dissolve into every other.

This social and moral outlook now pervades public discussion. It is inculcated by educators, employers, advertisers, moral leaders, government agencies, electronic media, commercial mass culture, and in some cases the force of law. Even mainstream religion has come to reject natural, traditional, and transcendent standards, connections, and identities in favor of technocratic ones. Christian love becomes a matter of encounter, inclusion, accompaniment, nonjudgmental support, and promotion of social administration for utilitarian and egalitarian ends. Older standards, which had to do with the maintenance of the familial and communal arrangements by which people lived, and thus accepted the systems of identities that articulated those arrangements, are seen as ugly, irrational, bigoted, and worthy of suppression rather than discussion.[1] Under such circumstances the proper meaning of America, the West, and even Christianity become their own dissolution. That conclusion follows from a technocratic way of thinking, now considered simply rational, that denies the legitimacy of distinctions that define traditional particularities. Such a way of thinking harmonizes with the scientistic belief that modern natural science is the only source of knowledge, and the liberal belief that equal freedom, viewed as an open-ended principle that defines itself in ever broader ways, should be the supreme social and moral goal. It has become all but impossible to argue against regardless of its actual consequences.

## Totalitarian liberation

A liberal technocratic system needs workers, investors, consumers, and functionaries, and makes use of them in accordance with their wealth, organizational position, and certified competencies. But it has no use for traditional identities and arrangements like religion, sex distinctions, defined family forms, and inherited cultural community, which it sees as irrational and profoundly at odds with the purified order to which it aspires. Such things must therefore be discredited and rendered nonfunctional, and the populace turned into an aggregate of interchangeable human resources. Eliminating their effect—what is called fighting discrimination and exclusion—has thus become ever more prominent as a progressive cause, along with promoting mass immigration, defining family, religion, and sex distinctions out of existence, and denying the value and increasingly the very reality of historically evolved cultural community. We are told on authority, for example, that there is no such thing as Western civilization,[2] or Swedish[3] or French[4] culture.

In service of these goals, the identities that support and articu-

---

1 Spadaro and Figueroa, "Evangelical Fundamentalism and Catholic Integralism in the USA," discussed in chapter 4, exemplifies this attitude.
2 Kwame A. Appiah, "There Is No Such Thing as Western Civilisation."
3 Kajsa Norman, "A Very Swedish Election."
4 Yves Jégo, *"Emmanuel Macron et le reniement de la culture française."*

late traditional connections—male, female, American, Catholic—need to be suppressed. That is difficult, because people are attached to them, so what is done is what liberal society has done with religion: agree that traditional identities are important for those attached to them, but insist that they have no legitimate public significance, and everyone can define them for himself as he wants and insist on equal acceptance and respect for his own idiosyncratic and possibly subversive definitions. The trans woman, the gay Christian, the Muslim woman in a hijab as the true American, have thus become iconic figures. In contrast the white American and "fundamentalist" Christian have become objects of hatred, contempt, and fear. Their practical connection to our country's history is too close to ignore, and specific national histories, populations, and identities threaten the project of de-nationalization, so they must be denounced as demonic. Their very existence makes people feel unsafe.

Similarly, the family is redefined as a freeform personal project that the state may recognize to the extent it suits its purposes. The American "gay marriage" cases,[5] which treat marriage as a pure legal construction, make that clear. So the family may survive in name, but it is no longer the basis of society. Its substance, the duties spouses owe each other and the authority and obligations of parents toward their children, are simply what government says they are. Otherwise everyone is free to do as he wants: a man can marry a man, a wife can turn into a husband, marriage can be dissolved at will, and if a teenaged girl wants to get an abortion or mutilate herself with "gender confirmation" treatment, he, she, or xe can do so with institutional support and without parental consent or even knowledge.[6] Objections to this are considered purely a result of hatred.

## Unequal equality

People must understand themselves somehow, and they do so largely through the eyes of others and what is important to them.

---

5 United States v. Windsor and Obergefell v. Hodges.
6 Smith, "Gender Reassignment Surgery Is Now Available to Oregon Minors Without Parental Consent."

In the current climate, personal identity—what people think they really are and their reasons for valuing themselves—comes to depend more and more on one's relation to large liberal institutions. Since market and bureaucracy are the only social arrangements that matter, identities based on bureaucratic position, money, and lifestyle gain ground at the expense of traditional ones.

Everyone with talent and energy therefore becomes a careerist, because career is how you "make something of yourself." The compulsion penetrates everywhere. The wealthy are no longer content to form a leisure class, but are convinced they need jobs for their lives to mean anything. Women have few or no children because it would interfere with the careers that they believe give them substance as human beings. Children mean giving up one's identity; trying to become assistant vice president for sales apparently does not. Scholars become bureaucrats and intellectual entrepreneurs who are judged first by their conformity to ideological demands, and then quantitatively, by influence as measured by number of publications and citations, and by the grants they bring in. And nearly all princes of the Church are unwilling, even when old age and retirement put them beyond serious personal consequences, to speak out against outrageous conduct within the Church when doing so would damage their institutional standing. How can they break with a lifetime of pursuing their careers in an environment that treats organizational interests as ultimate? To do so would betray all they have been.

But careers do not make people equal. In the end, they establish a vanishingly small class of the successful who run everything. All others are their underlings, and in one way or another are viewed as failures. And even the successful are slaves to the system that made them and can unmake them.

## Servile freedom

Liberalism promised liberty, beginning with freedom of speech and political participation and expanding to include freedom of lifestyle and self-definition. It has destroyed those liberties by trying to make them absolute, subordinating them to the practical requirement that we integrate ourselves into a system that supposedly vindicates them but is run by billionaires and bureaucrats who put their own interests first.

In the interests of safeguarding identities, the system effectively abolishes them by making them trivial. In theory we can choose what we will be, but when identity is deprived of all content and effect that freedom means very little. "Lifestyle choice" means that we put career at the center of our lives, which means almost inevitably that we will end our lives as failures, but are allowed in our spare time to have whatever hobbies or indulgences we want as long as they do not affect other people and are harmless to the system.

Severe limits are imposed even with regard to the freedoms of speech and political action that originally distinguished liberalism. To be tolerated you must be a thorough technocrat who takes only markets and bureaucracy seriously. If you say you are a socialist or a libertarian people will be willing to discuss your contentions, because you are only arguing for greater emphasis on one principle or the other. But if you say "France should remain French," "a trans woman is still a man," or "marriage is the lifelong union of man and woman," respectable people will be outraged and you may have trouble finding employment. And if you try to start a political movement in support of such ideas, you and your supporters will be crushed.

The net effect is the imposition of an all-embracing and windowless—and thus totalitarian—system on everyone and everything in the name of freedom, reason, equality, tolerance, and social peace.

## Illiberal education

If career and consumption are all there is, and free intellectual life is suppressed, the purpose of education and intellectual life becomes vocational training and the smooth functioning of the liberal system. For students, teachers, and scholars the system promises careers; for billionaires and bureaucrats it provides technical expertise, trained operatives, and compliant subjects. Those interested in the good, beautiful, and true lose out, as do those wanting an education that inducts them into a great tradition, but who cares about them? Their interests and concerns put them at odds with the smooth functioning of a technocratic system, so they deserve rather to be ignored.

Education and expertise are subjected at all levels to centralized bureaucracy, if only through reliance on funding, and the system of education and training absorbs more and more of human life. The full absorption of women into the paid workforce makes daycare and early childhood education part of raising children, and the demand for "experts" leads not only to mass university education but even to mass graduate study. The overall result is that young people are subjected full-time to institutional processing and propaganda from infancy well into adulthood in ways designed to turn them into graded interchangeable resources that are as useful as possible to liberal institutions. They are still influenced by their parents and others outside the education, childcare, and pop culture industries, but more weakly than in the past, and the people exerting influence have also been formed by liberalism. At the same time alternative centers of cultural and intellectual life are starved of support.

The effect of this system is cumulative and overwhelming. Questioning liberalism becomes an incomprehensible attack on basic social reality and everything our contemporaries have been taught to hold sacred. It is also an attack on the life history, personal identity, social affiliations, and dearest hopes of everyone who matters. And it would mean relying on institutions like family, Church, and traditional community, culture, and identity that are less and less functional, have fewer and fewer grounds for claiming authority, and so hardly count as institutions.

# 9

# Political Correctness

Political correctness is an important aspect of the current destruction of thought and disruption of everyday life. Several decades ago, when it first attracted attention, conservatives tried to laugh it off and liberals denied its existence. After all, how could something so much at odds with reality and common sense be real? Today, though, its demands keep multiplying and enforcement becomes ever more rigorous. It has turned out to be very real indeed. That is the pattern in the advance of progressivism: what once seemed absurd soon becomes arguable and eventually unquestionable.

### Nature

"Political correctness" most often refers to demands regarding language. You cannot talk about illegal alien prostitutes; you have to talk about undocumented immigrant sex workers. But it is more than that. Progressives promote it in the name of equal treatment and respect regardless of who you are and how you live, while conservatives decry it as part of the campaign to suppress traditional culture and identities in the interests of a more bureaucratic form of social life. The two characterizations are substantially equivalent, since a system that guarantees equal treatment and respect for everyone regardless of identity makes it impossible for traditional identities and hierarchies to function, and that means bureaucratic management of the everyday details of life.

Either way, the demands of political correctness are far-reaching. It requires us to consider every way of life and configuration of personal qualities to be as good as every other in all respects.

Otherwise, our evaluation of people, at least in some settings, will be related to who they are. So prostitution must be spoken of simply as work, and illegal aliens as people whose presence in a country has not yet been registered and validated. Similarly, our speech must reflect the belief that men and women are the same, Muslim belief and practice are never a problem, and every 17-year-old in Los Angeles—even if he is "struggling," "academically at risk," or "inadequately served"—can be taught trigonometry and quadratic functions.[1] If we do not believe all that, then some people will be viewed less favorably than others in some connection, and that is now considered a moral catastrophe.

The point of "political correctness" in language is to make the way we speak conform to correct political understandings, so that incorrect understandings become impossible to express and eventually unthinkable.[2] The biggest problem with it, apart from the system of compulsion behind it, is that the "correct" understandings are false and destructive. People and groups differ in many ways, some of which matter a great deal. Men and women, young and old, Arabs and Japanese, all behave differently in ways that are often significant. To some extent political correctness admits the point, but tries to defuse it by "celebrating diversity." All special qualities are beneficial, or so people pretend. If someone has an ethnic or religious connection, or configuration of sexual habits, and feels it as part of who he is, we must view that as purely positive for everyone in every setting.[3] Such attitudes are obviously nonsensical. Differences can be either beneficial or injurious in various respects, and it is silly to pretend otherwise. As things are, however, the evident falsity of PC beliefs strengthens their social authority by ruling out discussion and obliging us to simple-minded support. Anything short of unquestioning adherence, which includes using correct language, means you claim the right to compare, distinguish, praise, and blame. That is the very definition of discrimination, and it makes you a bigot.

---

1 Duke Helfand, "A Formula for Failure in L.A. Schools."

2 That was, of course, the function of Newspeak in George Orwell's *1984*.

3 For a vivid example, see Heather Mac Donald, "The Corruption of Medicine."

It is also worth noting that the rule of equal respect does not apply to people who occupy different positions within liberal institutions such as corporate bureaucracies. In form it may be observed—people may refer to the CEO by his first name and HR materials may speak of the lowliest underlings as "associates"—but the lack of formal distinctions means a system of pretense that makes subordinates less sure of their ground and so less able to draw lines and resist abuse. And when progressive scapegoats are involved, such as white Southern fundamentalists, not even the forms are observed.

## Effects

The consequences of political correctness cut to the very roots of social life. In principle, it destroys culture as such. That may not be obvious, since it insists on equal respect for cultures and so claims to foster them all. In fact, though, insistence on comprehensive equal respect kills culture, making a tolerable social world impossible.

Culture is basic to society. If we are to cooperate effectively, most of what we rely on each other to do must go without saying. Culture enables that by giving us a common understanding of what the world is like, what life is about, and how people should act. That allows complex systems of mutual reliance to exist. Since man is social, culture enables him to be human. The objectionable feature of political correctness is not the need to accept the presence of existing minority communities and treat them decently, but the insistence that minority status should never make a difference. If minorities are distinct, the distinctions inevitably matter, and trying to suppress them does no one any good. Black community life got worse in the wake of the civil rights movement and the institution of affirmative action,[4] which systematically stripped communities of their most talented members; and the descendants of Mexican immigrants, raised by pop culture, the welfare state, politically correct schooling, and the consumer society, get into far more trouble than their parents

---

4 Garrett and Putnam, "Why Did Racial Progress Stall in America?"

and grandparents did.[5] Old social connections and controls disintegrated, and new ones failed to establish themselves.

The problem is not that some cultures are better than others, although they are in many ways. It is that culture is particular, and whatever the culture some people will not be part of it because their background, habits, and attitudes are inconsistent with it. Political correctness tells us that, as a fundamental command of social justice, everyone must be included and his outlook and habits receive equal consideration in every setting. That principle would require Peruvians to be equally included in rural Japanese society if any should choose to go there—as is their right. It would be exclusionary to subject them to an environment in which a culture not their own is assumed, for example, in which people assume that the equinoxes should be celebrated as holidays. The result is that such celebrations and the cultural assumptions behind them would have to be eradicated. The same applies, of course, to all special features of every society everywhere. The obvious consequence is that it becomes impossible for culture to function. How can codes of manners, ideals of sexual conduct, standards regarding family obligations, or expectations of reliability in this situation or that carry any weight when they differ among different peoples and each version must receive equal respect?

Since culture orders the human world, the result of attacking it is to plunge that world into chaos. Attempts can be made to fill the gap by ever-more-comprehensive systems of regulation and control, but a system of rules involves cultural assumptions, so such attempts inevitably fail. The social problems resulting from imposition of cultural diversity, for example through immigration policy, are often blamed on "exclusion"—resistance by majority populations to multiculturalism. This is absurd. In spite of the rhetoric about celebrating diversity, abolishing cultural authority is no way to promote peaceful and productive social life. People's desire to maintain the personal and cultural net-

---

5 Joshua Breslau et al., "Migration from Mexico to the United States and Conduct Disorder: A Cross-National Study." Also see Eric Berger, "English Linked to Promiscuity in Hispanic Teens."

works that give them a tolerable way of life is natural and praiseworthy, however opposed it may be to official ideology.

Even progressives accept special measures to preserve a threatened minority culture, but every such culture is locally dominant somewhere—otherwise it could not exist as a culture—and every culture is a threatened minority culture from a global perspective. So the distinction makes no sense. From the standpoint of diversity and tolerance, then, it seems best to accept efforts to preserve all cultures, including Western ones.

## PC culture

In fact, of course, political correctness does not really destroy all culture, since no society could function without some system of common habits, understandings, and expectations. Instead, it destroys traditional culture and replaces it with a makeshift pieced together from political propaganda, advertising images, attempts at social management, industrially produced entertainment, and half-baked therapeutic concepts.

Politically correct culture thus receives its content from the needs, workings, and governing assumptions of today's commercial and bureaucratic institutions. It has ideals, such as nondiscrimination and self-realization, and saints and martyrs, such as George Floyd and Martin Luther King, Jr. It gives life a goal through careerism and moderate hedonism, provides diversion and a form of community through sports, popular entertainment, the cult of celebrity, and attacks on dissidents, and allows us to pursue transcendence by taking permitted pursuits to extremes, as in the case of extreme sports, rigorous political correctness, and the higher consumerism.[6] It is not entirely uniform. People have different hobbies, professional biases, social enthusiasms, sexual orientations, tastes in pop culture, and so on. Such things affect their attitudes, habits, expectations, and networks of connections. As long as each of the resulting subcultures is PC, each recognizes each other's legitimacy. But they share common

---

[6] The latter is manifested in the wine and food mysticism on display in the very successful and actually rather good films *Sideways* and *Babette's Feast*.

weaknesses, since each must constantly undermine itself to avoid complaints about exclusion—that is why we see articles about how hiking has a diversity problem—and none reflects a sufficiently broad experience of life to substitute for an actual historical culture as a guide to living.

What all versions of PC culture share is opposition to natural and traditional distinctions, such as sex, cultural heritage, and religion, that are neither necessary to liberal institutions nor reducible to purely private tastes and satisfactions. Those indoctrinated into it find it genuinely revolting to give weight to such things—in their words, to be racist, sexist, homophobic, transphobic, religiously bigoted, and so on. Rejection of such distinctions and the ties they reflect is basic to their identity and sense of legitimacy as human beings. They feel infinitely superior to the bigots who cling to such things, to whom they feel little or no obligation of justice or humanity.

## The great awokening

For a long time political correctness found it difficult to attack traditional culture in a comprehensive way. It could not simply carry its traditions forward, because this would be to assert the distinctiveness and value of a particular culture and thus the people who produced and sustained it. But as the outlook of an elite class that claims superior knowledge and perception, it could not at first ignore, reject, or belittle the high culture and systems of professional ideals and standards that did so much to define that class as an elite.

The solution was to bend professional standards and ideals to include more women and minority group members, to pay more attention to their particular concerns, and to turn high culture against itself and against the larger cultural complex it expresses. So professional schools and organizations introduced affirmative action, and a system of dogmas and taboos developed around sensitive issues. The point of high culture became transgression against its own traditions and against human nature, both of which had come to seem tyrannical limitations on the will. *Regietheater*, which lets directors stage operas and plays with changed time period, geographical location, casting, plot, and stage directions, often in order to make some left-wing political point, is an obvious example.

Eventually, though, bending standards, re-interpretation, and subversion were not enough, and the time came to eradicate past culture, including past elite culture, more thoroughly. That project is now going forward in the form of "woke" ideology. This might be defined as "the belief that (1) all of society is currently and intentionally structured to oppress, (2) all gaps in performance between large groups illustrate this, and (3) the solution is 'equity'—proportional representation [without] regard to performance."[7] This outlook carries forward the PC agenda, but makes it more ruthless and single-minded, and adds an extreme emphasis on the evil of existing society and the immediate need for radical change.

Its time has indeed come. All significant social institutions, from the Department of Homeland Security[8] to the American Mathematical Society,[9] now pay homage to it. The most prestigious organizations and institutions tell us that fields of activity as varied and demanding as music,[10] museums,[11] and medicine[12] must all be transformed so that racial "justice" becomes their focus and their personnel and leadership become equally representative of all groups within the population. Similar attitudes apply with regard to other traditional dimensions of human identity, such as sex. While race is generally the primary concern, the same principles get adopted for other human distinctions. So it is now accepted that there are no significant differences between men and women, and all differences in result—in numbers of engineers or whatever—are a direct consequence of sexism. To say otherwise is misogyny. Under such circumstances, in which

---

[7] Wilfred Reilly, tweet, August 21, 2022.
[8] Christopher F. Rufo, "Department of Homeland Security Training on 'Microinequities.'"
[9] See, for instance, search results for "racism" at www.ams.org.
[10] Heather Mac Donald, "The Revolution Comes to Juilliard."
[11] Heather Mac Donald, "The Guardians in Retreat."
[12] Heather Mac Donald, "The Corruption of Medicine."

crude politics dominate everything, there is no real place for high culture or professional ideals and standards.

One reason for the seemingly irresistible power of wokeness is the difficulty of contesting it in public discussion. Consider education as an example. Currently, the mean SAT score is 1112 for white students and 934 for black students.[13] What do such figures show? According to prominent scholar Ibram X. Kendi, university professor, Guggenheim fellow, National Book Award Winner, MacArthur "Genius Grant" recipient, and *New York Times* best-selling author, they simply show the pervasiveness of racism. His explanation of the point[14] presents woke logic with great clarity: "Either there's something wrong with the test takers or there's something wrong with the tests. . . . There's something wrong with the test. . . . And to say there's something wrong with Black and Latinx children is to espouse racist ideas." Respectable mainstream people do not dispute the point, and the result is a growing movement away from testing of any kind. The same kind of argument applies to grades, discipline, graduation rates, and other areas of school life where there are major long-standing racial differences in results.[15] So we also see attempts to transform these other areas. The burden is on educational institutions to make sure everyone ends up in the same place.

Similar arguments apply to all major social institutions and relationships. For example, the 2020 FBI figures give a black person as the offender in 57% of the murders for which information is available,[16] even though black people are only 13.4% of the population.[17] The figures for London, where most black people in

---

13 See reports.collegeboard.org/sat-suite-program-results (accessed September 2021). There seems to be a tendency to make such information less available. See Scott Jaschik, "College Board Will Not Make Public AP Data by Race."

14 Ibram X. Kendi, "There's something wrong with the exam school tests—not with Black and Latinx children."

15 Brandon McCoy, "Closing the Racial Achievement Gap."

16 See crime-data-explorer.app.cloud.gov/pages/downloads.

17 See www.census.gov/quickfacts/fact/table/US/RHI125219#RHI125218. I use the 2020 figures, rather than the 2021 figures that show an even larger black share, because the latter include fewer police departments.

Britain live, are remarkably similar.[18] But what does that show? Those who share Professor Kendi's way of thinking would presumably say that the problem is with the police and their statistics rather than the facts on the ground.[19] The problem in black neighborhoods, it is said, is not criminality but over-policing and aggressive prosecution that makes crime rates seem higher there than elsewhere. That line of thought does not seem to explain murder rates, which mirror the number of dead bodies, but that discrepancy can ignored, obfuscated, or explained by the tendency of white supremacy to drive black youth to desperate acts. Woke thought has therefore led people to the view that the criminal justice system is thoroughly racist, so that prison has to be rethought, policing transformed, cash bail abolished, common misdemeanors decriminalized, and so on.

Wokeism has further complications. It is not clear, for example, how Asian-American SAT scores (average 1239 versus 1112 for whites) or the FBI's attribution of 88% of murders to men rather than women fit into the narrative of white patriarchal oppression through educational testing and law enforcement. And telling people that all their problems are the fault of other people rarely works out well. So far the main result of Black Lives Matter, apart from burned and looted buildings, seems to be more dead black people (along with some others).[20] People may feel compelled to defer to current social movements, in part because they want to keep their jobs,[21] but reality feels no such compulsion.

However, the general view seems to be that arguments over actual facts are a distraction from the burning need to correct horrific social injustice. Historical and existing societies display complexities that stubbornly resist change, such as unequal results for different people at the individual and group level. Since that situation is considered intolerable, everything that

---

18 Sky News, "Black Murder Victims and Suspects: London v. UK."

19 For an example of such thinking, see Hans Bader, "Washington Post Leaves False Impression about the Crime Rate."

20 Alexander, "What Caused the 2020 Homicide Spike?"

21 Ira Stoll, "List of People Canceled in Post-George-Floyd Antiracism Purges."

exists and everything that has ever happened is thought to be tainted—that is the meaning of "systemic racism"—and the remedy will necessarily involve rejection of history as a guide and abolition or radical transformation of all social institutions.

## Tyranny rising

It seems unlikely that the current effort to transform stubborn realities in the interests of equality will be more successful than the much more limited twentieth-century attempt to abolish economic inequality. But if no one stands up against a view, and a great many people push it forcefully, it is going to prevail, and people will try to put it into effect. So woke ideology and related developments are likely to have an increasing effect on the world in which we live. Suggestions that they are likely to prove a passing fad seem unreliable, in view of the breadth and depth of the forces behind them as well as the failure of similar predictions regarding previous outbursts of political correctness.

And that is bad news for anyone who cares about the common good or political, intellectual, and spiritual freedom. Wokeness makes the abstract principle of social equality absolute, and that means tyrannical suppression of normal social functioning. In pursuit of its demands it calls for comprehensive central control of social reality. People must be made equal, and how else can that be brought about? But that means enormous expansion of government to the point of effective abolition of personal agency, since if choices matter the results will be unequal. Among other things, attitudes and beliefs will have to be controlled. Political correctness means suppression of forbidden thoughts and those who harbor them. These are defined in ever farther-reaching ways, to the point that ordinary people cannot be trusted to make up their own minds on anything important. Worse, fences must be established around forbidden thoughts to eliminate stepping stones to "radicalization." The necessary result is rule by a small number of people who claim to have the superior knowledge, intelligence, and virtue needed to define what views are correct and what safeguards are needed.

In this and other ways the woke ideology that has grown out of political correctness reflects technocratic society in its goals and methods. It sets itself a single abstract and indeed mathematical goal, equality, and treats social institutions and human relations as technical means for maximizing that goal. Human beings and their lives are thus viewed as raw material and products of a social machine, and if the results are not what is wanted then redesign and tighter controls are needed. No place remains for independent thought and action. The social machine becomes all in all, so as in other totalitarian systems everyone and everything must assimilate or be crushed. The result is destruction of the complex system of goods that characterizes a normally functional society, and thus a sordid tyranny.

## Coolness

The human spirit always tries to find some outlet. Politically correct culture is deeply unsatisfying. It cannot deal with life as a whole because it only values aspects that fit the needs of dominant institutions. So it reflects the outlook of the young, ambitious, unimaginative, and relatively successful for as long as they keep their forward momentum, and has little except distraction and dissipation to offer other people. It thus ignores the heights and depths of human experience—love, loyalty, family, friendship, enmity, loss, defeat, aging, and death. Even for the young and ambitious it is inadequate, because it makes everything so thoroughly mundane. Something more is evidently needed to make life larger, more open-ended, and above all less boring. The pursuit of extreme sensation interferes with career. The refinements of consumerism rapidly become tedious. How many people can care that much about craft beer? The puritanical austerity of radical egalitarianism and the joy of crushing dissenters are too negative. And the narcissistic obsession with the details of one's self-defined identity that seems characteristic of many young people today, especially students at elite colleges,[22] cannot long be sustaining.

A makeshift remedy, but the best available within the liberal order, is provided by "coolness." Coolness seems trivial, but peo-

---

22 See Roberta Katz et al., *Gen Z, Explained: The Art of Living in a Digital Age*.

ple take it much more seriously than they admit. It started with jazz musicians, and still has something of the spirit of the night, of escape from everyday reality, of unconditioned freedom, of improvisation without a goal. It is the progressive equivalent of the divine grace that bloweth where it listeth and none can define. So it has something in common with sanctity. The cool are in the world but not of it. They possess a certain disengagement, so that they are independent of their surroundings and not easily excited or flustered. They are not conventional, and recognize immediately whatever they are presented with. That gives them a sort of perfect pitch in matters of perception, expression, and practical decision.

Of course, coolness is also very different from sanctity. Sanctity is about eternity, coolness about now. It has implicitly religious aspirations, but its hedonism and individualism mean they go nowhere. The lives of the saints have enduring interest because they point beyond themselves; the lives of the cool do not. Its lack of content allows coolness to eke out an existence in the spiritual world of progressivism, even though it puts it at odds with the heavy-handed compulsory moralism of political correctness that may someday destroy it. But lack of content is otherwise a radical defect. It makes coolness a matter of style: that is why a clumsy but determined attempt to be a saint is admirable, while a similar attempt to be cool is ridiculous. At bottom, of course, it makes no sense. It is notoriously unsustaining, and those who live by it either fall into gross hypocrisy ("sell out") or grow out of it. Within the liberal order, though, growing out of it means growing out of the only thing, other than sex, drugs, celebrity, moral posturing, fanaticism about sports, food, and other trivia, or lots and lots of money, that redeems life from quotidian dullness. It means turning into a boring, conventional, older person, just like Mom and Dad.

# 10

# A New Order?

In the previous chapter we touched on how the destruction of traditional culture means its replacement by a new PC culture. A broader and more detailed discussion is needed. What kind of culture is it, how does it work, and what kind of life does it offer to those who are part of it?

## Progressivism as a faith

Nature abhors a vacuum. To carry on life with any confidence we need to feel connected to the order of the world in some definite way, so that we will be able to place ourselves and understand how to act. That is why modern secularization has led repeatedly to extreme political and social movements that promise a substitute for the traditional social and spiritual order. The great totalitarian movements of the twentieth century provide examples.[1]

A society must have a faith that sustains it. Until recently it was obvious to everyone that at least an informal establishment of religion is necessary. It was not until 1905 that republican France took crucifixes out of schools and law courts, replacing them with the Tricolor. East Asia is considered secular, but China was purportedly ruled by the "Son of Heaven" until 1911 and Japan by a living god until 1945. And in America the Supreme Court asserted as recently as 1952 that "we are a religious people whose institutions presuppose a Supreme Being": up to the 1960s, the public school day in America normally started with prayer or Bible reading.

---

1 Robert Nisbet, *The Quest for Community: A Study in the Ethics of Order and Freedom*.

The insistence on religion was entirely rational. To understand their own actions, people need to understand their position in the world and how their actions connect with it. Otherwise, action is pointless. We would be living in the world according to Samuel Beckett, and we cannot look at our lives that way. This requirement is not only individual. Something as all-inclusive as a society could not function without broad agreement on ultimate principles. The industrialization of social life and expansion of state responsibilities to include childcare, education, healthcare, social welfare, and even the reform of social attitudes make that need more acute and comprehensive than ever.

Since something is needed to lend ultimate sanction to schools and courtrooms, when Bibles and crucifixes are taken out something else soon comes in. Ten years after the Supreme Court said Americans were a religious people, the justices banned prayers and Bible reading from the public schools. These were soon replaced by Martin Luther King Day and celebrations of diversity, to which rainbow flags and Black Lives Matter banners have now been added. A political and social regime considered secular has thus revealed itself as still faith-based, but in a perverse, non-theistic way. Hence political correctness and all the candlelit vigils and other observances. And hence the abusive treatment accorded to skeptics and dissenters who refuse fully to sign on to the project. While present-day society supposedly values freedom and diversity of opinion, it suppresses dissent and imposes nonstop indoctrination. To oppose progressivism is to oppose what is understood by progressives as fundamental moral reality rooted in the nature of things. That is seen as wrong, ignorant, dangerous, and indeed incomprehensible. It threatens the very social order. How can it be allowed?

Progressivism is a jealous god. As in other societies, fundamental political and moral principles take precedence over lesser considerations. Science and learning must therefore come to progressive conclusions; when they do not, scientists and scholars can face serious consequences. Traditional religion must also get in line. Fundamentally, progressives view it as an irrational and disruptive force. They accept individual and private spirituality as a sort of hobby or psychological therapy, but insist on keeping religious faith out of social and political life except to the extent it serves to poeticize progressive goals and principles. This exception offers religious organizations an opportunity for renewed relevance and legitimacy if they replace their original substance with progressivism itself. In its mainstream forms, Christianity has therefore become all about inclusion, accompaniment, and progressive social justice.

The transformation appeals to many religious leaders and "respectable" believers, who want to cut back on the personal demands of their religion, whose disciplines and doctrines they no longer take seriously, while adding to its public respectability. But the result is that progressivism itself becomes the substance of their faith. It tells them what life is about, defines the means of salvation, has saints, martyrs, rituals, doctrines, and demons, and persecutes blasphemers and heretics. When such people are dominant, as they usually are in mainstream religious institutions, the institution becomes a particular rite within the universal Church of Progress. Its faith as traditionally understood gives way to psychological therapy and social betterment, and "mission" comes to mean promotion of secular social progress, especially elimination of racism, sexism, homophobia, and so on. Forms and language are mostly carried forward, but the meaning and content is quite different and converges on secular progressive thought.

## Its strengths

We have pointed out the weaknesses of the system of thought that now dominates the West, but it has its strengths. Its great strength is that its principles—whatever the logical gaps—are clear, simple, and forcible, lend themselves to effective systems of propaganda and control, and tell us with few ambiguities what to do and how to do it. Their extraordinary success transforming Western life is proof enough of that. Its principles also align with the active, enterprising, domineering, and anti-contemplative—and therefore ultimately mindless—spirit guiding modern life. They legitimize ruling institutions like global markets and supposedly neutral and expert transnational bureaucracies; indeed, they make them the only institutions with legitimate authority. After all, if you do not accept equal preference satisfaction through material and social technology as a supreme standard, you must hate rationality or want to injure people whose preferences differ from yours. Such is the progressive view, and why should the people who hold it tolerate the bitter clingers, irredeemable deplorables, and semi-fascists who reject it?

## Its weaknesses

But the progressive faith cannot give rise to a culture that sustains people. The people may not have a good theoretical response to what they are told, but they stop listening to the slogans, trusting the authorities, and showing up at the woke churches and political rallies.

## The new identities

The effort to free us from subservience to social identity inevitably fails. We are social beings who understand ourselves largely by reference to how others understand us. We identify with what we take pride in, but need that to be something others recognize and respect. A deep weakness of the new order is that it offers no good way to satisfy that need.

At one time people felt pride in family, because families stood for something. The same was true of nation. People felt they could take pride in being Greeks, Romans, Spaniards, or Englishmen. Their country and people seemed to stand for something admirable—courage, good sense, independence, the ability to rule, and so on. And above all it was their own and a legacy from their fathers. That pride served a social function because it provided something to live by that connected people to each other and to the arrangements through which social life was carried on. Today the looseness of traditional connections makes that kind of pride seem out of place. People assume that practical life should be carried on through bureaucratic or commercial arrangements like daycare centers, fast food restaurants, and insurance companies, and only distinctions that relate to such arrangements should matter. But then why take pride in being an Englishman or even care about it? As the response to Brexit showed, the enlightened believe that taking such distinctions to heart is stupid, pointless, and bigoted, and can lead only to conflict.

## A New Order?

From their earliest years people today spend their lives mostly in bureaucratic custody. The things they take seriously they mostly do with colleagues, fellow students, and the like rather than family and other non-commercial and non-bureaucratic connections. The result is that ideals of life and standards of conduct come less from the communities one is born into and more from peer groups, colleagues, pop culture, official propaganda, and therapeutic professionals. That is why we feel freer to speak of generational differences—differences due to changes in pop culture and the official party line—than sex or ethnic differences. The former make sense to us, the latter are felt as an embarrassment that we should deny or at least avert our eyes from. In such a setting, career, wealth, educational background, and ideology are what people take seriously, so they place themselves by reference to them rather than traditional identities. It is not acceptable to think you have a place in the world because you are a white man, but it is acceptable to think so because you were educated at an elite institution, are doing well in your profession, and have approved tastes and views on social issues. The politically progressive young professional who is rising in his career and knows all about cooking and craft beers has become the upper middle class social ideal.

The importance of such matters is demonstrated by the ruthless pursuit of career, the obsessive competition to get into the most prestigious schools, the endless signaling to demonstrate correct political alignment, and the increasing tendency to cut off family relationships on account of ideological conflicts. It means that in America we are willing to accept rule by the Supreme Court, an unelected committee that in recent decades has been composed almost entirely of Yale and Harvard alumni. Such people are thought to have the right to rule because of their expertise and institutional position, and that is considered entirely consistent with our supposedly democratic public order as long as they have the right ethnic and sexual balance. The rise of "international human rights"—an idealized image of the featureless social world our rulers want—as a legal norm that hands over the most basic social decisions to transnational elites and bodies similar to the Supreme Court indicates that other Western countries are increasingly imitating that arrangement.

## Their failure

People want the self-respect that comes from being something definite that accords with an ideal. In a world ordered by technocratic institutions, the only way to achieve that is to distinguish oneself professionally, though perceptiveness of consumption choices, and through devotion to "equality"—that is, by helping destroy the importance of traditional goals and connections and confronting people who think they matter. But those ways of establishing identity are useless for most people. Career success depends on talent, luck, and a great deal of effort. Most people fall short in some or all of those respects. Few can climb the corporate ladder, and institutions such as Yale and Harvard exclude almost all applicants for the sake of defining a small ruling elite. So only a minority find career aspirations a usable guide to life.

Nor is political correctness any better. It is hard for people who are not devoted careerists or their hangers-on to see the world from the ideological perspective now favored, since that perspective mostly has to do with running the system of top-down social management that the current understanding of "social justice" requires, and dividing up promotions and the perquisites of office—hence the obsession with "glass ceilings" and so on. And competitive consumption cannot sustain many people, because it is expensive, and because "perceptiveness" is pointless unless it is limited to a few people. Young people in protected academic environments can occupy themselves piecing together complex subjective identities on campus and on social media—demisexual vegan ecological warrior or whatever—but is that something they will truly be able to live by?

So current trends leave ordinary people without a system of life and identity that works even minimally. Many become anxious, confused, depressed, isolated, and increasingly non-functional as they fall prey to addictions, distractions, resentments, and other self-destructive behavior.[2] It is possible such people will pull together and turn to something better, like a serious and grounded form of religion. The easier course, though, is to con-

---

2 See Charles Murray, *Coming Apart: The State of White America, 1960–2010*.

tinue the slide, or turn obstinate and rebel, most directly through vehement assertion of some aspect of traditional identity. In the absence of a grounded overall conception of social order, such assertions are likely to either dissipate or go too far. That is one reason respectable people, who see no justification for traditional identities or particular loyalties, think of Nazism when they see the success of Brexit and Donald Trump. After all, what motive could there be for emphasizing national identity, in a world in which it seems to be losing its function, other than narrowing the circle of human concern and defining those who fall outside it as unworthy and threatening?

Even for the successful, the current system has its problems. Identities that have a function in progressive society—those based on career and social views—do not run deep. Career success can disappear overnight, and it has a notoriously amoral quality that makes it a poor basis for a satisfying life. The latter point can be remedied somewhat by working for a progressive NGO or the right government agency, or otherwise using one's position to advance progressive goals. Professionalism can also help, since professional standards are a socially recognized ideal. People can take some pride in being a doctor, lawyer, teacher, or so on, and even being a chef has acquired prestige. But the effect of such aids is marginal, and professional standards are always subject to the criticism that they are cloaks for white supremacy and the like.

Correct social views create solidarity with those who are admired and powerful, and license abuse of dissenters, but they are otherwise not personally rewarding. Displaying them is mostly a matter of voting, signing petitions, saying the right thing, and otherwise signaling progressive attitudes. Unlike honesty, loyalty, charity, chastity, and the whole array of traditional virtues, these things do not much affect how someone carries on his life. And both career and political correctness can involve a certain slavishness that does not sit well with self-respect.

Above all, a view that resolutely excludes basic human realities from consideration leads to private unhappiness. It results in a way of life and system of personal and social ideals that is unable to deal with the situations in which people actually find themselves. Careers reach dead ends, politically correct ideology offers few personal satisfactions, and all lives are unsuccessful in worldly terms, since they end in weakness, loss, suffering, and death. So the current combination of careerism, consumerism, political correctness, and social climbing is humanly less functional than a way of life oriented toward enduring goods and relationships ordered by a system of identities. For all its material wealth, the current system cannot even produce the children it needs to reproduce itself.

That is one reason there is so much ill humor today: people try hard to do what is thought right, but when they succeed they find they do not much like it. That is also why virtue signaling and online lynch mobs have become so prominent. People feel the need to pump up the rather insubstantial qualities on which they base much of their claim of personal worth by turning aggressive and intrusive. Hence the intolerant moralism of woke politics, which sees itself as burningly righteous and resistance as beneath contempt, and hence the emotional charge words such as "racist" and "homophobic" carry, and their ever-broader range of application. Such attitudes reflect a desire to distinguish oneself based on distinctions that are humanly unrewarding.

## Identity politics

Identity politics are useless as a response to this situation. They seem to provide a way to establish a place for oneself in a featureless technocracy,[3] but the place they establish does not help anyone carry on his life.

People want to be able to take pride in such traditional aspects of identity as sex, religion, and inherited cultural community. These are basic features of human life that do not go away when their functioning is disrupted and they lose social credit. So people find ways to retrieve something from the wreckage. They feel entitled, for example, to take pride in success that represents progress. The financial and occupational success of a woman or black person simply as such is considered a legitimate reason for

---

[3] Mary Eberstadt, *Primal Screams: How the Sexual Revolution Created Identity Politics*.

pride. It makes him or her an icon of how the world should be, and the achievement a standing assault on social injustice. The point can be extended. An obese black lesbian can take legitimate pride in her identity as such, because simply by existing, and still more by asserting herself and her identity in every possible setting, she confronts patriarchy, white privilege, fatphobia, and heteronormativity.

This search for pride through opposition has a political function. Diversity multiplies inequalities, misunderstandings, mistrust, and resentments. Progressive politicians appeal to the pride of their supporters and to real or supposed injuries in order to stir them up against their opponents. The maneuver is disastrous for peaceful cooperation and social happiness, but not entirely unprincipled. Progressives want to destroy the function of traditional forms of identity, but when minority and traditionally subordinate groups assert their own traditions vigorously, traditionally dominant identities can no longer order social life. So minority assertiveness actually does promote the progressive version of equality. Even so, identity politics is not personally rewarding. Its point is not to provide a sustaining way of life but to undermine how others live. The only joy it provides is the joy of opposition. And few people can build much of a life on that.

# 11

## Political Paralysis

There is very little hope that the current situation can be retrieved by ordinary political means, since our political life is in the grip of the same institutional, social, and intellectual trends as everything else.

### Triumph of the strong

Given free rein, the subjectivism that today's thought promotes would destroy public order and indeed public reality. That cannot be allowed, so its consequences are restricted to accommodate the needs of the governing classes, and thus subordinated to their desire for a stable, efficient, and easily administered society. That is why the Supreme Court applies its proclaimed "right to define one's own concept of existence, of meaning, of the universe, and of the mystery of human life" to abortion but not tax evasion. The sole remaining objective standard for determining what can be treated publicly as real and important is thus the institutional interests of the strong, who in our society are a mixture of billionaires and bureaucrats, the latter including media, academic, and legal functionaries.

This situation has made politics a matter of social management for the sake of economics and popular compliance. Matters that fall outside the class and institutional concerns of the strong, like family, religion, local or historical community, and traditional forms of identity, are therefore removed from politics. Where possible they are treated as subjective matters of purely private interest that cannot, it is said, be allowed to matter socially without violating the autonomy of the individual and disrupting public life—meaning, among other things, orderly rule by money and bureaucracy.

## Fascism

But law and politics must be tied to principles able to inspire obedience. The bare convenience of the powerful cannot do that. So what principle can be put forward? And where does it come from in an individualist, materialist, and subjectivist world?

We need a principle that tells us what to do. The need is rational as well as emotional. Part of rationality is acting in accordance with a principled understanding of our situation and what it makes sense to do in it. So if reason is the same as modern scientific thought, and we want to be rational actors, modern scientific thought has to tell us what it makes sense to do. It appears it can do so through the principle of following preferences, since our preferences tell us what to do. They are observable, and Occam's razor tells us not to multiply entities beyond necessity, so it seems most scientific to stick with them. Preference satisfaction thus becomes the *summum bonum* on which politics and morals should be based.

But that presents a problem, since preferences clash. What pleases you may displease me, and how can it be determined who gets his way? The most obvious solution to the problem is what looks like the most realistic one, saying that what takes precedence is the will of the strongest. If you want to know what the authoritative social rule is, you find out who is in a position to force his rules on everyone. If people accept that principle we will have social peace—that was Thomas Hobbes's insight—so we should all submit to it. So we are back to the will of the powerful as the inevitable social standard in a materialist world, supplemented by an appeal to the need for peace, the most fundamental of public goods.

To strengthen the approach, so that a principle that still seems inadequate can inspire obedience, a method consistent with the appeal to strength is helpful. The obvious method is for the strongest to put their determination of social standards beyond question by showing their superior strength in as undeniable a way as possible, for example by arbitrary and abusive treatment of others. Then no one will dare raise questions, and the standards laid down will become unquestionably valid. That approach defines ideal fascism. It has usually been dressed up with marches, slogans, uniforms, athletic displays, a mystique of action, struggle, or the State, appeals to historical glories, superiorities of blood, or the Darwinian law of survival, and so on.[1] The Nazis followed it in the most energetic way possible by combining campaigns of conquest, enslavement, and extermination with a constructed mythology involving ancient Aryans and archaic symbols like runes and swastikas. Those who identified with them obeyed for the feeling of power, purpose, adventure, and solidarity it gave them; those who did not obeyed out of terror (when given the choice) or paid the price.

In spite of its often archaic symbolism, fascism was no less modern than today's progressivism. As such, it accepted modern tendencies such as the emphasis on technology and on absolute human autonomy, in the form of the principle that the will of the Leader is the highest law. But it differed from progressivism by trying to limit individualistic and leveling tendencies and restore drama and comradeship to political life by emphasizing some concrete non-economic institutions like the nation, and virtues like courage and loyalty that do not reduce without remainder to equality and utility. The evident thought was that doing so would focus and energize public life and thus reverse the disintegrating tendencies of modernity.

It also re-emphasized certain traditional identities, but in a non-traditional way that absorbed them into the state and turned them into a system of ranks with definitions, privileges, and disabilities that often had little to do with their historical evolution and function. Thus, the "Aryan Race" had only the vaguest connection to evolved historical realities, the "unity of the German people" erased a complex system of regional identities in the interest of a military and bureaucratic style of organization, and sexual standards were systematically manipulated and maternal

---

[1] The historical forms of fascism were quite various, so much so that it is often difficult to say which movements qualify, but the term is useful for referring to a basic tendency of modern thought and social organization, and I will use it as such in the way indicated in the text. The same is true of "liberalism" and "socialism," which I use to refer to forms of egalitarian hedonistic technocracy—that is, progressivism—that differ mainly on the expediency of markets.

and child care bureaucratized to produce more Aryan warriors—that is, raw materials for a wholly modern military machine.

Fascism thus tried in a brutally simple way to deal with the problem that man does not live by bread alone but must, in order to inhabit a moral world, have a definite place in that world and something greater with which to align himself. But it had serious fundamental defects. In the absence of a genuinely transcendent principle to make sense of the system as a whole and the relative function and importance of its parts, it based itself on pure assertion and favored the combative virtues above all others. It had no principle of balance, and ultimately disdained utilitarian calculations, so the triumph of the will that is the goal of modern politics generally became the triumph of aggressive willfulness. That ended badly.

## Progressivism

Reason and experience show that the fascist approach, however brutally realistic it might seem, cannot last. Man is a social animal, and any man can kill any other—that was another of Thomas Hobbes's insights—so no one is strong enough to dominate a society for long without the willing cooperation of its people. Cooperation is based most easily on people's understanding of what benefits them and how the world should be. So a system of cooperation requires a principle people can be persuaded to accept as beneficial to themselves. Modern propaganda techniques are effective, but need something to work with, and progressivism serves the purpose. All desires and choices, it notes, are equally such. So if they are to be the basis of morality and politics, then equally furthering all of them, subject to considerations of efficiency, consistency, reliability, and so on, seems a uniquely rational political and moral standard. Morality and politics then become a matter of social technology in the service of egalitarian hedonism.

Everyone can find something to like in that view because it seems to give him what he wants. The weak are happy because it seems to put the social order at their service and give them equality with the strong. The strong accept it because it gives them an organized society and compliant populace to work with, and they will be able to determine the concrete application of its principles. And the bored, who might prefer the excitement of fascism, can be mollified by the promise that each can follow his bliss in his own way, and, if they are idealistic, by the ascetic challenge of self-transformation that is required by progressive standards of radical equality and inclusion. Hence, for example, the popularity of Black Lives Matter in mainline white churches: it adds something that seems demanding and transformative to the lives of bored and comfortable middle-aged people.

## Similarities

Progressives see fascism as their great opponent because it opposes them from within modernity. That is why today's progressives believe that if you are not one of them you must be a fascist: we make our own world, so politics is necessarily a matter of the triumph of the will. The only question is whose will it will be—everyone's equally or the will of some particular group and leader. They cannot imagine a third possibility, because they cannot imagine rejecting something as basic to modernity as the arbitrariness of valuations.

Even so, they find it impossible to avoid some fascist tendencies. For example, progressivism cannot avoid using the convenience of the powerful as an ultimate criterion, because maximum equal satisfaction cannot be computed and in practice requires simple subordination of the preferences of some to those of others. My desire to have a loud party at 3 a.m. conflicts with your desire for a good night's sleep. Bob's desire for acceptance of his recently adopted identity as a woman conflicts with Mary's desire for a women's locker room free from naked men. What does the principle of equal respect for arbitrary choice require in such cases? It does not allow them to be resolved by reference to the human realities that man is diurnal and has two sexes that differ profoundly in ways that include female sexual vulnerability. After all, Bob and I evidently reject such claims, and we have an equal right to define reality.

So the disputes can be resolved only by flipping a coin, or by reference to the efficiency, stability, and coherence of the system. The latter are basic interests of the powerful, and they provide the standard that is chosen. Since it is in the interests of the people who run things to have well-rested workers, noise ordinances are generally acceptable even though some people are night owls. And traditional sexual standards and identities support loyalties and ways of life our rulers do not control, so violating them is permitted and indeed applauded. The result is that I cannot have my party, but if Bob says he is a woman he can hang around naked in the locker room while the middle school girls' swim team is using it. More generally, the freedoms and satisfactions we are allowed are those that fit neatly within the progressive system: career, consumption, and lifestyle choice, all from the menu of options thought harmless or beneficial to our rulers. If I decide instead to do one of the many things now considered antisocial, for example call publicly for would-be women like Bob to be kept out of the ladies' locker room, I am increasingly likely to face social and professional penalties.

Liberal progressivism thus establishes its own form of arbitrary regimentation. Progressivism claims to be based on neutral reasoning—that is the basis for its claim to be uniquely non-oppressive—but neutral reasoning is rarely enough to resolve practical issues. The interests of the powerful or arbitrary choice masked as expert opinion must therefore play a decisive role. I have mentioned imposition of transgenderism as one example. Responses to the COVID-19 pandemic, which often seemed motivated less by intelligent analysis than by the desire to appear in control of the situation and a general prejudice in favor of a society organized on industrial lines, provide others. Why, for example, are churches, which were subject to lockdown, less essential than liquor stores or the homosexual hook-up app Grindr,[2] which were not? An even more obvious instance of arbitrariness was the refusal of public health authorities to shut down Pride Month "social" gatherings or even issue clear warnings of specific dangers at the beginning of the monkeypox epidemic.

Liberal progressivism ends up committing to irrationalism in other respects as well. It is ultimately based on purely individual

---

2 Peter Hamby, "Baseball? Coachella? Handshakes? Tinder? Anthony Fauci on the New Rules of Living with Coronavirus."

interests, so it cannot justify sacrifice. It can tell us why the system should favor equality, but not why any of us should make that goal his own. Why act as a progressive, except to the extent one gets something by it personally? Liberalism has no good answer. The need to defend a system that depends on commitments it views as irrational obliges progressives, like fascists, to answer objections by abusing and silencing dissenters. As with fascism, that approach can involve definition of privileged and subordinate identities that line up somewhat with traditional identities but lack their traditional functions, serving as battle flags or insignia of rank rather than guides to life. Thus, BIPOC and LBGTQ+ people are now favored over sexually normal white people because favoring them resolves disputes while degrading the authority and functioning of traditional arrangements.

The license granted by progressivism to bullying can be a source of short-term strength. One motive for progressivism today is the pleasure of identification with the powerful who run the system and abusing the deplorables who harbor doubts. The progressive habit of calling opponents "fascists" thus involves a great deal of projection. Communism, a radical form of progressivism, displayed that tendency with utmost clarity. It was progressivism in a hurry that early adopted the features that were to characterize fascism, such as blatant lies and brutality, partly for the feeling of power and comradeship they confer, and partly for the sake of a more effective struggle. Our own liberal form of progressivism is more moderate. It involves some of the same methods and motives, but has so far generally contented itself with censorship, slander, social shunning, firing, and connivance at mob violence.

## Progressivism and power

Modern politics has settled into managerial liberalism as what appears to be its terminal state. That system is integrated with the way people do everything today, and it is very hard to fight pervasive social reality or even step back from it far enough to see it as something that might possibly be changed.

The system is based on simple understandings. Liberals see

themselves as uniquely rational, and identify rationality with technology and modern natural science, so they treat those practices as fundamental. They see government administration as a way to establish the authority of trained expertise. As such it establishes basic order, regulates markets, defines rights and obligations, promotes equality, secures personal and social well-being, and manages conflicts among changing and increasingly chaotic social forces. At least rhetorically they treat contract as almost equally fundamental. They see it as the basis for relationships among individuals, such as what they still call marriage. It gives them the market, the most effective mechanism for producing wealth and multiplying consumer choice. And they see it as a source of political authority to back up the authority of expertise, through a fictional but theoretically necessary contract that joins particular wills into the social will that animates government.

In spite of their supposed commitment to the social contract and therefore the popular will, liberals also use government to correct people when they fail to act as liberal theory says they should. They appeal to democracy rhetorically but have always had an uneasy relation with it. Democratic voting ties political measures to the will of the people, in line with the view that will is the source of moral and political obligation. But it also means that the minority must accept the will of the majority—a very serious inequality. Nor are voters reliably sensible or progressive. They can be short-sighted and self-centered, and often do not understand the facts or the likely consequences of their choices. They can also be manipulated, especially in an electronic age that dissolves reality into a whirl of images and soundbites that can be reassembled to tell any story whatever. And they may value illiberal things like traditional identities or close and enduring human connections. So their choices cannot be relied on to support the system or to maximize equal freedom or even their own benefit.

The result is a movement away from voting and consumer choice and toward decision-making by supposedly expert bureaucrats. People still talk about democracy, and in theory the people should be given what they want, but they must want the right things. Progressives have faith in neutral expertise, especially their own, so they think it obvious that they should filter information and supervise discussion so that people will make the right choices, and establish other safeguards to mitigate the effects of wrong choices. So consumer choice becomes thoroughly regulated, and voting a temporary check on serious decisions rather than a normal way of making them. When votes go the wrong way, as in the case of votes against the EU or in favor of Donald Trump, established institutions cooperate to minimize the consequences, and then re-educate voters so that next time they vote the way they should. If need be, thumbs are put on the scale to secure the right result.[3] These tendencies conform to a technocratic vision of social life that now seems incontestably correct to most influential people. They also give businesses and other powerful interests and institutions an opportunity to exert influence behind the scenes and so ensure that government actions are consistent with their needs and desires. Society is run more coherently and efficiently, and so benefits from the standpoint of its basic governing principles. These tendencies should therefore be viewed as basic features rather than corruptions of contemporary liberalism.

## Conservatism

Many people have viewed conservatism as a defense against the destructiveness of liberal modernity. But conservatism can conserve very little, because it lacks the overarching perspective needed to distance itself from the established regime. The result is that it cannot be anything but yesterday's progressivism. The mainstream conservative response to today's identity politics, a rehash of the classical liberal and individualistic view that traditional dimensions of identity should matter as little as possible, provides an example. Identity is a central political and social issue today. The conservative response—at least in America—is to say people should ignore the issue. What good does that do?

---

3 See Molly Ball, "The Secret History of the Shadow Campaign That Saved the 2020 Election," and Mollie Hemingway, *Rigged: How the Media, Big Tech, and the Democrats Seized Our Elections*.

## Maintaining continuity

At its least theoretical, conservatism simply engages in foot-dragging. That may provide some temporary restraint, and promotes at least short-term continuity, but cannot work for long.

A somewhat more principled approach was that of the original neoconservatives, who were chastened liberals who wanted to make their fellow liberals more realistic. They proposed that a progressive society requires non-liberal elements, such as family, religion, and communal loyalties, to remain stable, sane, and functional. So they favored patriotism, praised the free market for promoting prosperity and personal discipline, and generally supported a mild social conservatism that permits natural law, religious tradition, and traditional forms of identity to have some effect on attitudes and social life. That strategy did not work either. Liberalism is progressive, and eventually rules out every non-liberal value and institution regardless of consequences. So neoconservatives had to give ground continually and eventually conceded every point at issue in order to remain part of the public discussion. All that remained was advocacy of a forceful foreign policy.

## Restraints on "progress"

Other conservatives put forward particular demands that seem likely to restrain progressivism. Thus, constitutionalists believe government should act only within the limits of the powers agreed to by the people in a written document. As discussed below, this approach delayed but did not stop the advance of liberalism in America. In the long run, people who run things interpret constitutions, like other laws, in the way that makes most sense to them.

Libertarians say rather that government should leave people alone. If everyone looks after himself and his own, what happens will make sense to those involved, and popular tradition and natural law will be allowed some effect. That approach sounds good to ordinary people who do not like the way they are governed and want a simple solution. It sounds especially good in America, where there has always been an emphasis on limited government and individual and local initiatives. The problem is that libertarianism is an inadequate theory of government. Like constitutionalism, it unreasonably expects government to self-limit. Also, it treats law as the basis of social order, but allows it no role other than protecting property and contract. When libertarian principles have made headway, the effects have been to weaken public concern with personal morality—for example the functioning of institutions such as the family—and to extend the free activity of markets by promoting globalization, big-box stores, and fast food franchises at the expense of local and traditional arrangements. Those effects in turn have led to more comprehensive systems of government involvement to deal with the damaging social effects of pure market rationality. So libertarianism has generally defeated its own stated goals, and declined as an intellectual movement.

Populism is pure popular rebellion against liberal modernity, especially its technocratic form. At bottom, it is a popular vote of no confidence in those who run things. The basic thought is that everything will be all right if we just get rid of the weird things the higher-ups have been pushing and get back to normal life. This approach has severe limitations. Numbers give ordinary people immediate influence when they are aroused and active together, but it is hard for them to compete with full-time professionals. They are not reflective, certainly not collectively, so their views are usually poorly articulated and their goals shifting and inconsistent. They lack organization, leadership, and vision, and cannot develop them without ceasing to be populist. Beyond that, their way of life and ability to act collectively have been disrupted by industrial society, consumerism, the welfare state, electronic entertainment, political correctness, and demographic diversification. The result is that populism gets distracted, loses focus, and wins only temporary victories. Referenda on social issues—affirmative action, gay rights, assisted suicide, and so on—provide examples. Socially conservative populists won the initial votes, but progressive judges, administrators, media figures, and educators determined their effect and undertook re-education campaigns that eventually brought the people around.

## Social conservatism

A problem with both populists and libertarians is that they want to get rid of the defects of the liberal order by adjusting the power of its components rather than changing its principles. Libertarians want to leave everything up to the individual, while populists want to put ordinary people en masse in the driver's seat. In each case those favored are expected to follow their own interests and inclinations, and that, given the correct distribution of power, is supposed to lead to better things. But why expect procedural changes to attract long-term political support and bring about substantive results that endure?

Social conservatives try to go deeper. They favor principles and institutions that are at odds with liberal modernity and therefore emphasize local, informal, and traditional institutions—family, church, local community, particular culture—guided by traditional standards and understandings that mostly have to do with informal attachments and people's sense of who they are, and of what is natural, accustomed, and ultimately good. In many ways they are similar to populists, but are somewhat more conscious of principles. Unfortunately, they have a hard time explaining their position even to their own satisfaction. The terms of public discussion today are modern, postmodern, and liberal, and offer no good way to articulate anything different. In order to participate in public discussion social conservatives have therefore accepted the basic principles of their opponents. They argue against "gay marriage" on grounds of religious freedom, against "affirmative action" on the basis of equal opportunity, and against abortion based on equality—that of the unborn child. But their opponents find such arguments absurd and indeed disingenuous, because they think it obvious that freedom, opportunity, and equality point in the opposite direction. So they have been able to offer determined and sporadically effective resistance on some issues, but overall have continually lost ground.

## Religious and intellectual conservatism

Religious and intellectual conservatives have tried to improve on that. "Ideas have consequences," they say, so they emphasize the errors of thought that have led to the current situation. But they have generally not gone far enough. Religious conservatives are loyal to heritage, and run into problems when their political and social heritage is fundamentally liberal. America, God, and freedom get mixed up together, and the easy way to deal with difficulties is to gloss them over and focus on symbols and rhetoric.

Literary and philosophical conservatives have tried to be more thoughtful. But they are scattered, and tied by professional commitments to an academic world that has become, in America, a half-trillion-dollar industry providing training, expertise, and propaganda to government and business. They have no social base, and are weakened by a personal and professional need for respectability that inhibits them from raising issues respectable people do not want raised. For that reason, they have focused too much on the ideal side of life, on vague appeals to faith, values, the inner check, the moral imagination, and so on, without enough attention to political and economic organization, the need for concrete authority, and touchy issues such as race, class, gender, and immigration.[4] Recently, for example, some prominent Christian conservatives, many of them associated with the magazine *First Things*, publicly proposed that universalistic principles need to be supplemented with particular loyalties, and equal freedom replaced by the common good as an ultimate social standard.[5] The proposal was rather vague,[6] but in principle it rejected basic aspects of liberal modernity, and that aroused vehement opposition from fellow conservatives. The concern for the common good reminded hoped-for allies of the Inquisition, and a group of Catholic and other Christian scholars, some very prominent, published an intemperate open letter associating par-

---

4 Those who deal seriously with these last issues from a non-mainstream perspective have generally emphasized natural-science considerations and shown little interest in literary or philosophical tradition.

5 Various signatories, "Against the Dead Consensus."

6 R.R. Reno, a prominent member of the group, proposes a re-emphasis on national community, and presents the proposal as a practical option in present-day public life, but details remain sparse. R.R. Reno, *Return of the Strong Gods: Nationalism, Populism, and the Future of the West*.

ticular loyalties such as nationalism with Nazism and denouncing them as "anathema" to Christianity.[7]

## Awkwardness about identity

That response points to a difficulty all forms of conservatism face today. Conservatism involves a desire to maintain social continuity and carry forward the heritage of the past. But the American past is intertwined with traditional understandings of identity. Worse, it is overwhelmingly European, and it is unclear how it relates to a country that progressive policies are making more and more diverse demographically. The result is that opponents increasingly identify American conservatism with sexism, homophobia, transphobia, xenophobia, and above all white supremacy, which is now considered the sin of sins and ever more broadly construed. Such accusations are impossible to shake off, and from the progressive point of view are plainly justified. Until conservatives find effective ways to respond to moral claims regarding identity that justify more traditional attitudes, their cause is hopeless. And it is very difficult for them to do so, because they want to appeal to an American and Western tradition that has turned against itself with regard to such issues. As a result, they feel an overwhelming need to show that their positions follow from those of Martin Luther King, Jr. But that cannot be done unless both conservatism and King's views regarding equality and what it requires are interpreted in an utterly unreal way.

## Other rightist tendencies

The failure of conservatism to respond effectively to the left has led to a variety of proposals for something more radical. These anti-progressive tendencies recognize that conservatism has conserved nothing, and range from neo-fascism to Catholic integralism to the diverse tendencies classified as "alt-right" or "neo-reactionary." These views, which mostly exist online, take a very critical attitude toward the American regime, especially its growing hostility toward natural and traditional identities, reject respectability and any serious desire to take part in mainstream

---

7 Various signatories, "Open Letter against the New Nationalism."

politics, and attempt to re-appropriate past political thought and apply it to changed circumstances to find an alternative to the current regime. Where they will go is unclear, and their criticisms of current trends are usually more plausible than their proposals for the future. But their writers are often intelligent, perceptive, and well-informed, and their lack of social or institutional position makes it possible for them to make obvious points on sensitive topics that no one respectable dares mention.

In spite of their frequent anonymity and lack of mainstream presence or institutional standing, they seem to be exerting a growing influence on disaffected young men[8] and on some more mainstream figures. The most-watched cable news host, Tucker Carlson, has picked up on some of their themes, the *New York Post*, largely under the leadership of Catholic integralist op-ed editor Sohrab Ahmari, on others. And the investigative journalism carried on by *Revolver News*, probably the most visible outlet that is generally aligned with these tendencies, has had noticeable effect on discussion of issues such as the January 6, 2021 riot at the Capitol. To a large extent, their influence has lain in broadening the range of topics and arguments it is possible to discuss in some public spaces, although the collapse of progressive thought into dogmatic insanity likely accounts for most of that tendency. The long-term effects of their activities are of course unknowable.

---

8 It is worth noting that in spite (or because) of a lifetime of indoctrination, one survey finds that almost half of Democratic men and almost two-thirds of Republican men under the age of 50 believe feminism has done more harm than good. Cassie Miller, "SPLC Poll Finds Substantial Support for 'Great Replacement' Theory and Other Hard-Right Ideas."

# 12

# Downfall

Why does the tendency of events seem so unshakable? Why do views that have such evident problems—that cannot ground loyalty or make sense of who we are or of thought itself—seem so obviously correct to educated and responsible people? And why, without a formal system of doctrinal authority, are progressive views developing ever faster, ever more in lockstep, and with ever less connection to reality? In short, what is the explanation for the strength and cohesion of liberal progressivism, why is it impossible for it to reform itself, and what will be the outcome?

## Petrifaction
Progressive orthodoxies have intellectual defenses that, in practice if not principle, make them all but indestructible. They are a black hole that people and societies fall into and cannot escape.

## A simplified world
The extreme simplicity of liberal modernity acts as a powerful defense by leaving few routes for attack. In current thinking rationality and morality are defined by technology and equal freedom. They tell us that other standards are irrational and immoral, and keep us busy with an endless series of tasks that prevent reflection. As time has passed, as liberalism developed, and as previous understandings dissipated, these views have become ever more dominant and their implications ever clearer. Technology and equal freedom work together as a system. That system is based on a few simple assumptions, so Occam's razor seems to tell us to stick with it. All we need to attend to is what people want, the relations among measurable observations—that is, to modern

natural science—and how to use the latter to bring about the former as efficiently and equally as possible. Everything outside those concerns, for example natural human goods other than simple preference satisfaction, is viewed as just another preference, and so reduced to the status of a private taste. But to give private tastes public effect is to impose arbitrary demands on other people. Why should anyone put up with that?

To be progressive is to take these principles to heart, and apply them single-mindedly. Hence the growing uniformity and dogmatism of progressive views worldwide, and the incomprehension and horror when someone disagrees with them even in minor ways. To oppose them is to oppose the freedom and wellbeing of humanity, and even reason itself. It is to appeal to irrationality and brute force. How could any sane and minimally well-intentioned person do that?

## Flawed rebellions

That way lies fascism, people believe, and the belief is comprehensible. Fascism might be defined as rebellion against progressive modernity through insistence on arbitrary assertions such as the right of a particular people to rule. As we have seen, it did not work. Irrationalism never does.

Other rebellions against progress and modernity have also failed. Reactionaries tried to return to a previous regime when that still seemed possible, often through the use of force, but did not take the modern challenge seriously enough, and in any case their time has passed. Romanticism rebelled against the soullessness of modernity and sought truth in poetic inspiration and strong feeling. But something beyond poetry and feeling is needed to articulate and stabilize the truths these uncover and tell us how they relate to other truths so they become definite and usable. So it too ended in failure.

More recently there have been less serious rebellions by anarchists, who reject technocracy because they reject coercive order, and various hippies, greens, feminists, and postmodernists who also tend in that direction. But their rebellion has been crippled by their failure to propose authoritative goods inconsistent with technocratic progressivism. The effect of their efforts has therefore been to strengthen the technocratic liberal state, which claims to be a neutral protector and facilitator of all tolerant ways of life, and so to promote what they thought they were fighting.

## Alternatives abandoned

The reason rebellions against liberal modernity have gone nowhere is that they have embraced ways of thought the modern conception of rationality excludes without proposing a different conception of rationality, making them irrationalist and thus unable to found anything solid. A successful rebellion—or rather counterrevolution—would require extending the concepts of rationality and objective truth beyond modern physics and technology, bringing mind, body, and spirit within a single system of understanding that does justice to all of them.

If the problem is that people are thinking about things the wrong way, it seems that the answer should be a reform in thought and education. Tell people to read Aristotle and Aquinas, for example, since these philosophers develop themes related to natural law, and encourage scholars to develop their thought as needed to deal with new situations. The Church once did that, but has generally abandoned the effort. Ever since the Second Vatican Council she has been emphasizing reconciliation with liberal modernity, and Catholic scholars have become much less interested in proposing alternatives to the latter. Saint John Henry Newman showed how to break with modernity and deal with the issues it raises while starting from an essentially modern outlook in his *Grammar of Assent*. Much earlier, Pascal had briefly sketched a somewhat similar approach in his *Pensées*. Both were based on pattern recognition: on reality coming into focus through consideration of infinitely many considerations that individually may say very little and often cannot even be separately identified. To understand the world by noticing patterns and how they work is to understand it through formal and final cause. But this attempt to bring back something of classical metaphysics also failed.

Nor have Catholics been alone in giving up. Many other people have proposed alternatives to modern ways of thinking that often seemed promising. The literary modernists—T. S. Eliot and

Ezra Pound are obvious American examples—were often skeptical of the modern project and favored other lines of development. But such efforts did not have much success, and have continued to lose appeal in recent decades. A few people may still find something other than liberalism or naturalism persuasive, but their views have no social or institutional footing, are rarely developed with much rigor, and are swamped by current orthodoxies.

## Practical entrenchment

Practical success makes political modernity seem plausible. It is hard to argue with tanks, Hellfire missiles, the Internet, modern medicine, the modern university, big journalism, big government and business, and trillions of dollars. Nor is it easy to argue with the physical comfort and endless possibilities of distraction modernity offers us.

People who run a mass industrial society with a mixed and fluid population find it easiest to understand their task in accordance with a general scheme that emphasizes technological rationality and maximum preference satisfaction. They have trouble making sense of traditional understandings of the world reflective of a more stable and rooted society. And their practice of throwing all humanity into a mass of interchangeable components to be integrated into a single industrial process results in acute public sensitivity to identity as different sorts of people jostle together. That sensitivity makes it necessary further to suppress traditional connections and identities in order to avoid disruptive conflicts. If there are too many Muslims, public celebrations of Christmas become impossible.

In any case, events seem to have discredited older understandings. The First World War meant an end to traditional and multinational monarchies, the Second to any serious European Right or strong conception of national sovereignty. Liberals and the Left had won, and their interpretation of events prevailed. These and other upheavals made the administrative machinery of the state all-encompassing, and destroyed local traditions and concern for standards other than effectiveness. The world wars were followed by the Cold War, which further centralized social life, increased government power, and made thought more ideological. Western governments became accustomed to social management based on grand slogans such as human rights.

The world wars were also followed by prosperity, TV, cheap jet travel, globalized markets, electronic communications, the contemporary welfare state, mass third-world immigration, and a continued tendency toward the industrial organization of life. People today eat at McDonald's, children grow up in daycare, young people live on social media, local establishments have been replaced by chain stores and the Internet, and our neighbors and colleagues come from all over the world. And with the collapse of Soviet communism, which before the rise of China and hardening of its political system seemed the last non-liberal form of modern political life, Western progressivism could unfold without an external reality check. How can a principle of tradition survive in such a setting? In what way are traditional understandings of identity relevant to the social institutions that now dominate our world?

Liberal modernity has thus won decisively. Whatever resistance some countries may offer, it is the only system that now seems capable of export. Fascism destroyed itself as a distinct system through violent irrationalism. Current hysteria about "fascism" is no more grounded in reality than early modern hysteria about witchcraft, although there are indeed irrationalist and dictatorial tendencies within all modern political systems. And socialism, including communism, was economically unsuccessful, so it disappeared as a distinctive approach to social organization. Even North Korea is liberalizing its economy somewhat, and its people are heavily dependent on technically illegal but tolerated private businesses for survival. When people speak of "socialism" today they mean giving bureaucrats more extensive powers within a liberal system that integrates private capital, which remains enormously powerful, with a government bureaucracy that in principle all consider omnicompetent.

As we have seen, conservatism goes nowhere. Communitarianism, eco-religion, and the more radical forms of feminism are even less serious. They are incapable of governing or even sustaining institutions. The same can be said of postmodern views that explicitly deny objective reality. The dynamic of modern thought leads in their direction, but it is impossible for people who run things to follow very far, since they need something that can give them a stable, efficient, and manageable society.

So liberal modernity has the argument from the lack of visible alternatives. Its supporters believe that their claim to be "on the right side of history" proves their position, or at least makes all other positions irrelevant. And in any event, non-modern and non-liberal political views have become publicly incomprehensible, their principles forgotten, their memory blackened, the traditional identities and institutions on which they depend the target of constant propaganda and all but nonfunctional. The result is that if you are not a liberal, a moderate (and therefore useless) conservative, or a leftist of a type people do not take seriously, you must be a fascist or insane. Such is the accepted view, and people can imagine no other possibilities.

## Self-destruction

It takes a long time for a new direction of thought to reveal its meaning. The Protestant reformers, their patrons, and the early philosophers of science did not know they were knocking the foundation out from under Christian Europe. They thought that if they made a few changes they would end up with an arrangement that served their purposes while sustaining a Christian civilization. And whatever literary and artistic critics might have said, industrialization and the rise of modern science and exclusively scientific ways of thinking were considered unmixed goods by those promoting them.

## Insoluble problems

The problems turned out to be greater than expected, and we now live in a social, political, moral, and spiritual order that has brought prosperity but in fundamental ways grows ever less hospitable to human life. Retreat seems impossible, and the power of the forces behind the direction of events makes it likely it will continue, in spite of the public and private miseries to which it leads, until practical circumstances make that impossible.

Modernity has been remarkably successful in what it cares

about: promoting wealth and power. Its intellectual life is highly institutional, and its institutions monopolize the rewards that facilitate recruitment of talent, so it has little practical intellectual competition. And the understandings on which it is based—identifying knowledge with neutral expertise, morality with maximizing the choices of individuals, and society with a sort of big machine—exclude sources of correction such as tradition, common sense, the *consensus gentium*, and recognition of everyday patterns. The result is that liberal modernity continuously radicalizes, loses touch with human reality, and feels obligated to destroy as oppressive all traditional and informal arrangements and distinctions. Once an advance is made on the road to equal freedom there is never any excuse for retracing it, and every step reveals deeper inequalities, irrationalities, and oppressions that must urgently be addressed. It cannot stop itself.

## The coming crash

The West is falling into crisis because it has rejected objective goods and stable identities as arbitrary and unfounded in the nature of things. The results of that rejection are catastrophic. If such things do not exist then *all* purposes and classifications are arbitrary. Man cannot be social or rational by nature, because he has no nature. But if man is nothing in particular, and human life has no intrinsic point, why is either worth taking into account? Rights and dignity founded in human nature vanish, and man becomes raw material for the projects of the willful and powerful. We end up with the situation now emerging, in which the world's people become an aggregate of unconnected individuals to be used and managed by bureaucrats and billionaires. The official alternative to such a tyranny is the divinization of individual man, based on the untrammeled freedom of individual subjectivity to define value and reality. That view is thought to define the moral order, and the Great Awokening seems to be strengthening it. But if it is taken seriously then reason and social order disappear. How far it will go remains to be seen.

The disruption of traditional forms of identity does enormous damage to private life. How can children grow up when there is no pattern of normal adulthood to grow into apart from pursuit of career, consumer goods, and private hobbies and indulgences? What happens to marriage in the absence of a settled and realistic understanding of what men, women, husbands, wives, and the marital community should be? Mutual agreement and implicit natural tendencies will no doubt be enough for some competent, balanced, well-intentioned, and generally successful people, but are they enough for a system people generally can rely on through thick and thin? The collapse of marriage among less successful Americans suggests they are not.

Putting private life aside, the atomized social world now establishing itself provides no evident basis for mutual loyalty or public spirit. What sense do those things make if they have no connection with who we are and how we think of ourselves? But without them, citizens will have little reason to stand by each other in hard times, or officials to work for the common good instead of their own private interests. Bare altruism, unsupported by conceptions of identity and natural obligation, is a weak reed to lean on. Again, sane, well-disposed, and comfortable people may continue to act well in most cases, but the world includes all kinds, and social arrangements people live by should be sturdy enough to stand up under difficulties.

Sooner or later, a view that abolishes any solid ground for human dignity and solidarity, and eliminates any conception of life in accordance with nature and reason, leads to radical dysfunction. Politics becomes irrational, manipulative, corrupt, and inefficient, with social peace dependent on threats and bribes. Rulers lose their grip, people stop relying on formal institutions, and eventually the official social order stops working and other arrangements take over. That was the sequence of events with communism, and it seems likely to happen again with liberalism.

Progressivism is rebellion against God, nature, and history in the name of human will. Thieves fall out, rebels even more so, so every part of the modern world is in rebellion against every other. Everybody hates existing realities—and increasingly each other. That is why there is no such thing today as a party of order, and "change" is the great political slogan. Left-liberals rebel against the greed and love of dominion unleashed by the liberation of the will, although they find it difficult to restrain those impulses in themselves. Right-liberals rebel against the smothering system of petty restrictions created by the cults of equality and expertise. Everyone else rejects both. They are told they are free, equal, happy, and empowered, but it is obvious they are not. They know something is deeply amiss, but no resolution or even clear identification of the fundamental problems of the system seems possible. And the abolition of objective reality as an ideal means suspicion, fantasy, and fear run rampant.

## What follows?

It is impossible to predict when a final crisis will come. The current system has shown itself remarkably adaptable, largely because its enormous wealth defers and softens all problems. And the collapse of an illusion or bursting of a bubble takes longer than those expect who see it for what it is. Everyday life has enormous staying power, if only because no one can imagine anything else. Hollow institutions keep on functioning after a fashion, however useless and expensive they become, if they play a basic role in how people understand the social order. The American system of higher education, which is expensive and unproductive but symbolically necessary, provides many examples. But if a system's fundamental tendencies are unsustainable, the longer the delay the more complete the wreck will be.

What will our situation be then? The collapse of current governing understandings is unlikely to lead to an immediate turn for the better. When a serious and sustained effort to eradicate the social relevance of something as basic as sex or particular cultural tradition falls apart, the immediate results are likely to be crude and unpredictable. Consider, for example, the situation in Russia after the fall of communism and abandonment of the attempt to abolish the profit motive. Our ultimate fate is likely to be similar but worse, because of the more fundamental nature of our error.

Fascism, as an attempt to impose social unity and order on some primitive basis through power, propaganda, and irrationalism, is sometimes suggested as a possible outcome. It seems unlikely, though, that when the time comes non-market and non-bureaucratic connections will be extensive enough to give fascism anything to work with. And we have noted its intrinsic instability. Most likely we have to look forward to something like the "Period of Stagnation" toward the end of the Soviet Union, eventually devolving as trust vanishes and institutions fail into a somewhat neo-Levantine society that carries on life through networks based on primary human ties and identities—family, tribe, religion—that reconstitute themselves when others fail, and possibly through militias and criminal mafias. That is where the radically cosmopolitan and therefore deeply fragmented society of the Middle East ended up, and it is not obvious why we should be different: as society dissolves, people anywhere will do what seems most likely to help them survive and carry on life coherently.

The result would then be a continuing decline in civilization as people withdraw into insular communities that maintain a certain coherence through refusal to engage others except in simple and immediately practical ways. Already we see signs of such a development in political correctness, the increasing ethnic and ideological rancor, the growth of class divisions and gated communities, the dissipation and corruption of high culture, and the apparent impossibility of productive public discussion among people with substantial differences of opinion.

# PART III

A New Foundation

# 13

# Changing Course

What can be done? How can a more stable, functional, and rewarding system of habits, attitudes, and identities be restored, so that life can be carried forward sanely and productively?

The obvious way forward is restoration of the West's Christian tradition. If what was imagined to be reform is not working, why not revert to what worked? Like other traditions, it has flaws and critics, but its contribution to civilization has been enormous, it has vast resources to build on; its missteps can be identified, reversed or mitigated; its critics have nothing better to offer; and for Christians the Christian tradition is indispensable. We are warned that the idea of reversing progress is absurd. And it does present difficulties, since Western and Christian traditions have turned against themselves, but we must go forward with what we have. A great tradition offers many possibilities, life is always teaching good sense, and people easily become attached to traditional identities and connections, so the materials are there. We cannot know the future, but the attempt to restore a great past has often been enormously productive even when what was restored was not an exact copy of the past. The Renaissance, which began as an attempt to bring back the culture of antiquity, is one example among many.

It is therefore possible that the West will return to sanity without extreme crisis. The evident power of the causes behind current tendencies, and the continuing absence of a turnaround in spite of rumblings and occasional outbursts of dissatisfaction, do not prove one will never come. Who knows whether a tipping point will come that could change everything? So we must try to change the direction of events and prevent the destruction of the basics of culture, which would likely be followed by a worse-than-post-Soviet collapse into chaos, tribal hatreds, and mafia rule. And if efforts continue to fail, we must still do what we can to maintain decency and rationality, prepare for crisis, and lay the groundwork for something better.

## Taking a stand

To change institutions and social practices for the better, people must recognize what is needed. Our most basic task is therefore to change ways of thinking. The system of traditional identities and institutions a tolerable society requires cannot be imposed but must be seen as the nature of things. Masculinity, femininity, marriage, religion, and particular community must once again appear as simply part of reality. This would require only a return of common sense, which consists in beliefs of the kind adult, functional, and socially connected people normally have about the world when not continually re-educated to believe something else. But such a restoration faces barriers in a public order that scorns tradition and pattern recognition as "bias" and "stereotype," and prefers formal expertise that systematically excludes normal human considerations.

People say that our public order wants to separate politics from religion, but that understates the case. It aspires to free public life—and eventually, since man is social, human life in general—not only from religion, but from nature and history. The goal is to liberate man by making him his own creator. That means an end to stable conceptions of natural law and human nature, and thus a continuing war against human identity. The effect, though, is that man becomes what those in power say he is. Western elites now claim the power to redefine at will the most basic human arrangements and understandings. Man has made himself God, and politics is the authoritative expression of his mind and will. So if you want to know about life and death, whether a baby is a baby before birth, or whether there are two sexes or twenty, you look to the political order and its authorized interpreters.

Changing that situation will require a transformation in how educated and well-placed people think about the world. But to understand that there is a problem with basic ways of thinking is already to be halfway toward solving it. And that offers hope. The forces of renewal have reality, common sense, and profound critiques of modernity to support them, and basically all thought, learning, and literature before the modern age. Against these there are inertia, convention, careerism, and institutional and class interests, along with lack of imagination and the bigotry, hatred, willful ignorance, and ideological tribalism that are required to cling to views that are obviously false and destructive and to abuse those who reject them. These are powerful forces. But the blinkered views resulting from refusal to recognize reality have never had rational credibility, and what credibility they had is dissipating as their consequences become more evident.

The result of this situation is that liberalism needs to silence opposition in ever more blatant ways in order to maintain itself. That is the reason for political correctness. In opposition, we need to speak as clearly and persuasively as we can, and never shut up. Our true audience is whoever happens to be listening rather than our apparent interlocutors, who may well be deaf to argument. In the end sanity will win, if not because of its persuasiveness then because of the self-destruction of its opponents. The danger, of course, is that their self-destruction will bring us all down.

## Contesting liberalism

Today's political ideals reflect a commitment to a technocratic society. Such a society is necessarily complex and hierarchical, and the way it must be managed raises certain difficulties. It requires detailed common understandings to coordinate efforts, but introduces cultural conflict everywhere by treating people with very different backgrounds as interchangeable resources. Maximum equal preference satisfaction presents itself as a principle that can establish the necessary common understandings in such a situation. It seems fair to all, has detailed implications that can be acted on, and seems to require very little in the way of positive beliefs. It even appears to let people retain their religion and culture, although they have to be willing to treat them as private pursuits. So it appears to offer everyone the best deal practically possible from the point of view of his own goals, and thus seems perfectly suited to serve as the uniting principle of a diverse technological society. And history, we are told, has borne out this view: the advances of liberalism have brought ever greater freedom, equality, tolerance, and prosperity.

## False account of man

The self-presentation of liberalism is misleading, and critics need to drive that point home. They should start by debunking the myth of progress and the propaganda about the horrors of the past and glories of liberation. To that end they should draw on exact scholarship and put together popular accounts that confront the false historical images on which public discussion is based. Much work has already been done, for example with regard to the imagined darkness of the medieval period, the claimed war between science and religion, the Black Legends about the Catholic Church, the supposed tolerance and enlightenment of medieval Islam, and the fabled glories of the great progressive revolutions. More work is now being done, as on the claimed unique evil of European colonialism[1] and of European civilization generally. This work must be continued and brought into public consciousness. And we need to expand the effort, for example, with regard to the history of family life and the sexes: is it really true that women are better off now than fifty years ago, or that the abolition of sex distinctions was the best way to deal with whatever problems there may have been?

But more substantive arguments are also needed. In particular, critics need to emphasize the contradictions and irrationalities of liberalism. We have seen that liberalism deprives people of definition by individualizing them absolutely. Its version of rationality is out of touch with reality, and its freedom, equality, tolerance, and pluralism are unfree, unequal, intolerant, and monolithic. Its perspectives are radically defective because they leave out basic features of life. They forbid us to recognize patterns, and force us into an understanding of human life based on mechanical cause and effect. As part of this, they define man as a creature of indi-

---

[1] See, e.g., Bruce Gilley, *The Last Imperialist: Sir Alan Burns's Epic Defense of the British Empire.*

vidual desire, so that his good consists in its satisfaction, and so treat him as asocial and indeed essentially amoral. But that is entirely unrealistic: we see ourselves not as sponges soaking up satisfactions but as participants in a social and moral world. Our goals mostly have to do with our relations to others, and we want to understand those goals as reasonable and right by some standard higher than our own desire. So the goals liberalism helps us achieve are not the ones we actually have. By concentrating on satisfying desire it fails to satisfy *us*.

Liberalism mitigates this last problem somewhat by calling mass rejection of higher goods "freedom and equality" and turning it into a supreme moral principle. Social order makes no sense morally if individual fulfillment is the highest goal—why should I respect it if my highest goal is my own fulfillment?—but it has a kind of sense if the goal is to promote individual fulfillment for all. Then those who run the system and their supporters can claim that their activities promote the dignity, autonomy, and chosen goods of every person. That offers such people the possibility of a life they can view as meaningful and justified, at least as long as they can claim their project works. But the solution does not give the people at large, who do not actually participate in running the system, a higher goal in life, or even allow them to have one. To be told, "Whatever you want to do is OK, as long as it fits in with the equally OK things other people want to do," will not support an ordinary person's sense of leading a worthwhile life. To the contrary, it tells him that the kind of life he is leading is no more worth leading than any other. That view is now authoritative, and it has gradually been pervading the everyday self-understanding of the people. Critics need to highlight its depressive and ultimately disastrous consequences.

## False freedom and equality

So we should insist that making equal freedom the highest goal leaves substantial questions unanswered. Freedom to do what? Equality in what respects? As we have noted, these questions will always be resolved by reference to the interests of those who run the system. Beyond that, to insist on the equality of lifestyle and identity choices is to deprive them of significance. It means that ordinary people are not allowed to take seriously the things they have always lived by. If someone praises the natural family, for example, because he has found it absolutely central to who he is, or believes it central to a humane and functional social order, he is implicitly criticizing some people and their preferences. That is now considered oppressive, since it forces such people to live in an environment in which such criticisms are treated as normal. So no ideal of how people should live together that is at odds with the liberal one can be expressed. People can say they are Catholics, Muslims, or anything else, but the practical implications have to line up with the views of liberal bureaucrats. In effect, they have to accept that their religion—their understanding of the nature of man and the world—is a matter of private taste rather than reality, which is defined for them by secular society. But then it can no longer be their religion. Liberal freedom and equality thus demand universal apostasy. They tell us that all are equal, but it turns out that some are more equal than others and must be treated as oracles whose word overrides ordinary people's deepest loyalties and convictions.

In any case, does the concept of a social system based on freedom and equality along with a pervasive system of regulation make sense? Liberalism proclaims equality but limits it by the need to provide economic incentives and establish an authority able to determine and enforce liberal standards. These needs can justify almost any degree of inequality in wealth and power. Further, the growing demands of equality with regard to lifestyle and identity limit freedom ever more radically. As things now are, students are indoctrinated against "microaggressions," fines are imposed for "misgendering," men are abused for "toxic masculinity," people go to jail for insulting George Floyd,[2] and Christian florists and bakers are assessed heavy damages for refusing to help promote "gay weddings." We must ask again and again how that can be called freedom.

---

[2] Josephine Harvey, "British Ex-Cop Jailed after Posting Racist Memes Mocking George Floyd's Death."

## Essential inhumanity

We must emphasize that progress along such lines diminishes people. Their choices, commitments, and identities are not allowed to matter, because the point is to equalize their consequences and keep them from affecting anyone else. The result is a custodial state that deprives ordinary people of agency, and of the functional ways of thinking now denounced as prejudice, in order to eliminate the danger that they will infringe on others' equal freedom. So people are told they are free, but not to be anything in particular, and their choices are limited to the menu of career options, consumer goods, and personal indulgences that the regime finds convenient to provide and manage. Such a life is not worthy of human beings. They atrophy morally as their social connections and responsibilities wither, so that their lives go downhill in a way described by Charles Murray in his book *Coming Apart* and in Britain by Theodore Dalrymple in his essays on the white underclass,[3] and dramatized by the recent decline in American life expectancy,[4] especially among non-elite white people.[5]

As liberalism develops, it thus reveals itself as a system that forces on unconsenting and increasingly uncomprehending populations inhuman beliefs that destroy the individual dignity, agency, and identity it claims to affirm. How can a system that denies human nature do otherwise? As these results become more evident, its rhetorical advantages can be expected to dissipate. It is important to encourage this process.

## The anti-modern alternative

A change in course is evidently needed. A stable system of traditions and identities is necessary for a rational and coherent way of living. The radical decline of such things means a decline in reason and order, so they must somehow be restored. But how?

---

3 Theodore Dalrymple, *Life at the Bottom: The Worldview That Makes the Underclass.*
4 Gina Kolata and Sabrina Tavernise, "It's Not Just Poor White People Driving a Decline in Life Expectancy."
5 Sabrina Tavernise, "Life Expectancy for Less Educated Whites in U.S. Is Shrinking."

## Views new and old

Moderns see human life as self-contained and self-defining. They reject its innate orientation toward what transcends it, and its necessary dependence on specific culture and natural features like the distinction between the sexes. Liberalism in particular treats us as featureless Cartesian egos inhabiting bodies and a surrounding world that can tell us nothing and that we are entitled to treat as a resource, like sand or gravel, for whatever purposes we choose.[6] On such a view, social life becomes a matter of the particular projects of individuals, and of the managerial and market institutions that reconcile and further those projects. To the extent that history, transcendent standards, natural human tendencies, and natural or evolved identities affect how we live, they are seen as burdens on human freedom to be suppressed or overcome. That is why "subversive" and "transgressive" have become terms of praise.

Even so, many people today, traditional Catholics and others, hold non-modern views that are far more adequate to reality, however difficult they may be to articulate in the current language of public discussion. These views involve a sense of natural law that bases politics on human nature. By nature, they tell us, man is a social being who comes together, starting with the family, in communities oriented toward common goods. These goods are rooted in innate features of human life, like man's social nature and sexual complementarity, so they are natural to us. Together with considerations relating to the way goods are realized socially, they define a natural law valid for all communities.

Natural law principles are too abstract to be the sole basis for community. They need to be reinforced by historical ties and other settled connections, and made concrete and practically usable through traditions of social and political life. The historic European nations provide examples of how that happens. Such

---

[6] Liberal concerns regarding ecology do not show the contrary. Among serious decisionmakers they are about maintaining the value of the world as a resource, and promoting global managerial bureaucracy as necessary to that end. Talk of Gaia and the like is decorative rather than functional.

arrangements evolve over centuries and realize themselves through particular institutions and identities—the Italian piazza, the English gentleman—that anchor various aspects of the local way of life. Abstract natural law thus becomes tied to concrete local institutions and evolved social identity.

These traditional views, grounded in natural law, imply that human life is not self-sufficient. A political community needs to be grounded in an authoritative overall understanding of man, the world, the purpose of human life, and what is ultimately good and true. Such an understanding cannot be seen as simply a human creation and remain authoritative. So a view based on natural law must be tied to religion as well as human nature and history; society must always have a religious basis.

In summary, modern ideologies relate to goals that in the end are very simple: desire and satisfaction in the case of liberalism; power, comradeship, and victory in the case of fascism. These goals are to be pursued in a straightforward technological way. In contrast, pre-modern views relate to complex hierarchies of goods interpreted through particular traditions and integrated with ultimate principles we do not fully understand. God, nature, and history define us rather than we them, and we need some knowledge of them and their mutual relationship to understand what we are and how we should live. We thus pursue our goods through ways of life and systems of belief to which we may contribute but which we cannot construct, and which tell us what we are.

## Putting the question

On all these points, pre-modern and non-liberal views are more reasonable because they include more of reality. But how can people be brought once again to accept them, when all respectable thought rejects natural law, human nature, transcendent authority, and traditional identities and standards as guides for how to live, in favor of free-form preference satisfaction?

Those who favor a more natural and rooted form of society are usually not combative or ideological. They just want life to go on sensibly in accordance with patterns and connections that are normally obvious to everybody. If other people deny something as obvious as sex differences or the value of functional local communities and the boundaries that make them possible, they are not sure how to continue the discussion. In contrast, progressives increasingly find such considerations incomprehensible. If you mention them today they complain about attempts to force values on people, stereotypical or "essentialist" thinking, or even hatred and fascism. They demand proof for every detail of every assertion; no proof is good enough, and your arguments never stick, so that the next time the issue comes up you will have to go through the same arguments all over again—assuming people are willing to talk to you at all.

## Making the case

To make progress, people have to be led to put aside the rhetoric of freedom, equality, and neutrality, and look instead at the kind of life they are being pushed into and the goods that motivate that kind of life. Then they should be asked whether those goods and that life are the best available. As social animals, for example, we necessarily play roles. Should the roles be technocratic or traditional? Should we be primarily employees, consumers, hobbyists, and clients of the state, continually supervised and re-educated by our betters to keep out of each others' way? Or would it express more of our humanity if we were primarily husbands and wives, French Catholics, English workingmen, or any of the other types traditionally recognized? These are difficult questions to raise, since they require people to step back from the now-ingrained belief in self-creation. But provoking such questions is absolutely necessary to get anywhere. Internet memes contrasting the "bugman" (a figure equivalent to Nietzsche's Last Man), or his feminine equivalent, to the "based Chad" (grounded and self-confident traditionalist) or "tradwife" (traditional wife, mother, and homemaker) hint at ways to dramatize the issue. But much more needs to be done, and much more thought and effort should be devoted to the problem,

One step toward moving discussion in a better direction would be to point to the universality of certain features of social life. If there is some practice or principle almost everyone approved of until very recently, such as sex roles or a sense of greater obligation to people to whom we are more closely connected by ancestry and way of life, it is very likely helpful in human life. If it is suddenly rejected, it is much more likely that people today are crazy than that everyone else ever was. Another would be to note that taking human nature out of politics means sacrificing goods necessary to a normal life to the ever more intrusive demands of abstract freedom, equality, and efficiency. Motherhood and the family, for example, are now sacrificed as ideals and to a great extent as practical realities to promote strict equality in career opportunities between men and women.[7] More recently, there have been attempts to abolish the very distinction between the sexes. Do such changes really make life better for people? Is career their sole interest in life and strict fairness with respect to the goods recognized by technocratic society their sole moral principle?

Another approach is to point out the oddity of the attempt to rationalize human affairs on industrial lines. Living systems, like men and societies, function in ways that are far too complicated to analyze fully. Their functioning varies by circumstances, and can be influenced somewhat, but for the most part follows innate patterns that must be respected. People can be vegetarians, pescatarians, or meat-eaters, but they cannot live only on celery, and no diet is going to cure cancer. If anything, our ability to transform social relations and other intangible aspects of human life is even more limited, because the conditions and patterns that affect them are so complex and subtle. For example, some societies have more crime or more great artists than others. We would like to reduce the former and promote the latter, but how? In a setting with so many imponderables a technological approach is useless. All we can do is try to understand and deal with human life as it is, by reference to living systems and their natural tendencies, ways of functioning, and implicit goals. That means relying on experience, good judgment, and general principles derived from long reflection on man's nature and good and the conduct of life—in other words, on tradition, practical wisdom, and natu-

---

[7] Patrick Fagan, "How U.N. Conventions on Women's and Children's Rights Undermine Family, Religion, and Sovereignty."

ral law. Such an approach necessarily relies on "stereotypical thinking," otherwise known as accepting the normal patterns of human life. That reliance is hardly irrational: the reliability of stereotypes is one of the most solid findings of the social sciences,[8] and it seems sensible to cooperate with normal patterns rather than denying them or trying to engineer them out of existence.

Beyond the oddity of rejecting natural social attitudes, patterns, and relationships, we need to point out the implications of the technocratic alternative now being forced on us. If human nature and natural law vanish, no purpose has a value superior to any other. It is all a matter of what particular people want, how to get it, and how to resolve conflicts. The only institutions that can claim authority are those, like global markets and transnational bureaucracies, that are based on preference satisfaction and universal content-free principles like equality and efficiency. It is hard to see what motives for cooperation such a system offers other than self-seeking ones like money, power, and fear of penalties. Abstract altruism may have some effect, but without more specific interpersonal ties than common humanity—which the abolition of human nature makes ever more insubstantial—how much should it be relied on?

We are told we should give the system our loyalty, because it sets each of us free to decide his own way of life. If you like your traditional family and religion you can keep them, and we should be grateful to liberalism for guaranteeing their availability. The claim, though, is absurd. We are rational and social beings who act in accordance with who we are, what the world is like, and what our fellows are doing. Family, religion, and ways of life need a basis in the nature of things, the attitudes of others, and our understanding of who we are to become something more than play-acting. Otherwise I could make myself a Druid, Jedi knight, or Assyrian nobleman by choosing the role and acting it out. But life is not a convention of role-playing hobbyists: we are all members of the reality-based community. If our social setting leads us

---

[8] See Lee J. Jussim, Clark R. McCauley, and Yueh-Ting Lee, eds., *Stereotype Accuracy: Toward Appreciating Group Differences*; and Lee Jussim, *Social Perception and Social Reality: Why Accuracy Dominates Bias and Self-Fulfilling Prophecy*.

to live like cogs in a machine who become lifestyle hobbyists in our down time, we will find it very difficult to think of ourselves more than fleetingly as anything else.

# 14

# Nature

Man governs himself to some extent, but he does not make himself. The question of human nature should therefore be at the center of rational political discussion. If political discussion took that question (and thus the question of natural law) seriously, it would have a reference point and some degree of direction and coherence, even though disagreements would remain.

## What is natural law?
Natural law is much the same, at least in basic concept, as what classical Western thinkers called life in accordance with nature, and classical Chinese thinkers the Dao (that is, the "Way"). We might think of it as a system of principles aligned with natural human functioning that aims at the kind of social and moral well-being that, like physical well-being, can in principle be understood and attained apart from revelation.

So it is a system that guides human life in accordance with our nature and good as knowable by experience and reason. People do not like that today, because they do not want to accept the nature of things as a guide. Modern physics treats nature as a mindless realm of atoms bouncing off each other in the void. People who accept that as their understanding see nature as a blind, oppressive force that tells us less how to live than what we have to overcome to be free. So they reject the idea of a moral law grounded in the nature of man. If innate differences between the sexes really are important, for example, what follows on this way of thinking is a progressive transhumanism that seeks to abolish the differences through biotechnology and social conditioning.

## Nature

If they are to accept the guidance of nature, people must be persuaded that modern physics does not describe all reality, and that meanings and goods are part of the basic structure of things. It is not difficult to show that modern physics has limitations. It cannot, for example, describe or explain itself. To tell us anything it has to mean something, but mathematical descriptions of particles in space cannot explain meaning. Nor can they explain biological functions, since these involve implicit goals. It is thus incapable of explaining human life. To do so we must see life as a system that comprises the material, historical, intellectual, and spiritual aspects of our being, but we have seen that the dominance of technocratic understandings, and consequently the terms on which public discussion is carried on today, suppress our ability to see the world in such a way.

Those who want a life in accord with reason need an adequate view of life and the world. Natural law is the obvious choice. It understands nature not in the sense of modern physics but in a sense more at home in medicine, where it refers to the normal healthy functioning of living things. Man, like other living things, has a distinct nature as a being of a particular kind. There are specific conditions that help him thrive, and characteristic ways in which he responds to situations and people. In particular, he is naturally oriented toward goods like health, beauty, knowledge, family, friendship, community, peace of mind, and higher things that enable him to orient his life and make sense of it. Such things are not simply a matter of personal preference, since they result from our identity as human beings and as social and rational animals, and our good is largely a matter of working toward them and bringing them into a harmonious system.

## Sex

Without such natural and evolved arrangements it is impossible to carry on life in a way that makes sense, and man becomes a jumble of inharmonious pieces. As an example, natural marriage integrates biological functioning, the sexual impulse, and the complementarity of the sexes with a variety of practical, emotional, social, and spiritual goods. Sex and the identities, institutions, customs, and restraints related to it therefore provide an example of the power of natural-law reasoning to explain human life. Unfortunately, they have also been found to display its practical insufficiency due to the disorder of moral life and thought in our day.

## Political role

Sex is basic to social order. That should not be a controversial claim, and it is odd that it has become so. Older political thinkers such as Aristotle viewed man as naturally social, and found it self-evident that society begins with the union of man and woman in marriage. Liberal thought in contrast begins with the individual, and constructs the state as his protector and supporter. The family then becomes a legal contrivance or a private contract among individuals, rather than a fundamental reality in its own right. That is the view that has led the Supreme Court to treat restriction of marriage to opposite-sex couples as irrational, and even as an attempt to harm same-sex couples.[1] After all, if marriage is a contract or contrivance to facilitate the projects of individuals, why should government facilitate the projects of some more than others?

Such views, while urged by respected voices, are at odds with reality. It is absurd to view marriage as a creation of the state when it existed long before anything like the modern state did, or as simply a contract when it is basic to the identity of family members. And how can the sex of the parties be irrelevant to an institution the point of which is to order sexual relations and integrate them and their natural consequences—most notably, children—into the general system of human life? The way to think about the family that best fits the place it has always held in human life is to view it as Aristotle did, as a normal, fundamental part of the human world, and concern ourselves with fostering and supporting it so it can carry out its essential role. That is the view of the Church, and it is the natural view for people to take who have not been indoctrinated into an ideology or addled by commercial pop culture.

Once that view is taken, the answer to current questions

---

1 United States v. Windsor.

regarding sex, the family, and the state fall into place. Marriage establishes a setting that is uniquely suitable for bringing new generations into the world. Families created through marriage provide people with social connections, enable them to bring a basic and often disruptive side of life into a humane order, help them through times of trouble, and care for the old, sick, and unfortunate. When marriage is weakened its practical functions become more and more the responsibility of government, which is ill-suited to deal with the problems of specific individuals. The result is that some needs are not fulfilled, others are not dealt with adequately, and costs continually mount.

The traditional view found in Aristotle thus aids our understanding not only of the family but of the state and its role. The natural authority of the family, and the need for government to supplement and complete it, explain how government can be necessary to social order without being its basis. Recognition of the family as a fundamental natural institution thus supports political authority while limiting it, and makes it easy, without the aid of dubious inventions such as the liberal theory of human rights, to avoid the extremes of anarchy and tyranny that plague today's political thought.

## Social setting

The question, then, is how marriage and the family can be supported as stable and functional institutions. The sexual impulse must be channeled so that it supports them and so becomes constructive rather than disruptive. That requires something like traditional sexual standards and identities. These are less a matter of rules, rewards, and penalties than of the meaning of sexual relations and our identities as man and woman, husband and wife. Man is a social and rational animal, which means that he acts in accordance with understandings of himself and his actions and situation that he shares with other people. Such common understandings are absolutely basic to social and moral life. So it matters what men, women, sexual relations, and marriage are thought to be. If marriage is to be something we can rely on, it cannot be a legal construction, sentimental celebration, or optional lifestyle choice whose content depends on the arbitrary goals of the parties. To be itself, it has to be understood as something definite and fundamental: as a union of man and woman oriented toward the natural consequences of such a union and based on distinct understandings of men, women, the relations between the two, their rights and obligations with regard to each other, and the nature and function of sex.

Given the importance of the relationship, as well as the strength and frequent waywardness of the sexual impulse, such understandings, while not based primarily on force or external discipline, must be supported by laws, practices, and attitudes that define marriage in a way consonant with its ends, and surround it with standards and expectations that guard and facilitate its functioning, for example, by treating it as the sole legitimate setting for sexual relations. And these standards must be treated as fundamental, so that to violate them is felt not merely as "breaking a social rule" but as betraying what we are as men, women, husbands, wives, and human beings.

## Social justice

Support for such arrangements is a matter of basic social justice. Sexual freedom and today's feminism deprive institutions on which we all depend of what they are due. That injures all of us, the weak and vulnerable most of all, so it is radically unjust. The argument for that view should be accessible to anyone who cares about people's lives. Sex is profoundly interpersonal and expressive, and it cannot mean what it naturally means and function in accordance with its natural design when set free from stable connections. If individual and social well-being are the concern, a healthy marriage culture is therefore a necessity. So a sane liberalism, one that valued freedom but wanted to avoid self-destruction, would not be libertarian on lifestyle issues any more than it would be communist on economic issues or anarchist on issues relating to public order. Just as it would accept the necessity of private property and a legal system backed by force, it would accept the necessity of marriage, the family, and something like traditional sexual standards and roles as specific institutions invested with social authority.

If we get rid of the natural ordering of the relation between man and woman, based on the function of sex and the natural meaning of the body, that relation becomes a matter of shifting, conflicting, and sometimes obsessive desires. We end up in the crude and manipulative world we see around us, with its hookups, incels, failures to bond, gender dysphoria, slutwalks, epidemics of STDs, and complaints about rape culture, along with a great deal of resentment and many stunted lives. Progressives claim to respect the individual, but their attack on traditional arrangements and identities destroys the dignity, respect, happiness, and effective freedom and equality they say they value. Traditional standards restrict what the people at the top and the commercial and bureaucratic institutions they dominate can do, and functional families diffuse authority to all levels of society and confer positions of dignity and responsibility on even the poorest. That is why the people at the top are social liberals, and it is why the age of liberation has been an age of ever greater inequality.

With that in mind, it is hard to see why people concerned about equity and human dignity should make common cause on sexual matters with billionaires and Hollywood celebrities. But the arguments presented above were put forward forcefully by the pro-family movement and failed completely. Their failure shows that they need to be combined with deeper arguments regarding social order, authority, rationality, and the nature of man and the world, and with practical action toward better ways of living. But more on that later.

## Nation

The need for particular inherited community and identities that link us to it provides another example of the power and insufficiency of natural law reasoning.

Distance and boundaries are losing their significance today. Air travel and container shipping make transportation far easier. The Internet makes everyone and every place equally close electronically. Traditional loyalties and identities do not matter when we surf the web, work for an insurance company, get our food from Whole Foods or McDonald's, or send our children to a school with staff and students from everywhere. So people increasingly think borders and inherited distinctions are irrelevant and disruptive. That is why many well-known Christian scholars, secure in their tenured positions in the bureaucracy of expertise, treat any sort of national or ethnic discrimination as the sin of sins and denounce nationalism as tantamount to Nazism.[2] Even the Jews, the gold standard for endurance as a people, now seem largely to be abandoning their traditions and intermarrying themselves out of existence.[3] And respectable British people were horrified when their compatriots voted for Brexit. Who wants to be shut up on an island with a bunch of lowbrow racist xenophobes?

## Particularism

An inherited culture is a system of cooperation developed through long social experience. There is no substitute for that process as a way of building up a system of life that works for most people in most settings throughout the whole of life. Without it we get weak human connections, stunted human development, and wrecked lives. And that is what we see around us.

Not everything can be run centrally or scaled up to global size. Our loyalties start at home and work outward, so we do not ordinarily feel a strong tie to others without some connection that is more specific than our common humanity. The networks of family, friendship, kinship, religion, and face-to-face community by which ordinary people live, and in which they find identity and dignity as participants, cannot be designed by experts or subordinated to a global system. When these networks weaken, people become isolated, self-seeking, and suspicious of each other.[4] And when public trust and cooperation disappear, so does (among other things) the possibility of rational public discussion. A perfectly cosmopolitan world would thus be an utterly irrational world ruled by force and fraud.

---

2 Various signatories, "Open Letter against the New Nationalism."

3 Uriel Heilman, "Pew Survey of U.S. Jews: Soaring Intermarriage, Assimilation Rates." The Orthodox, who reject many aspects of modernity, are an exception to this trend.

4 Robert D. Putnam, "*E Pluribus Unum*: Diversity and Community in the Twenty-first Century."

## Nationalism

For such reasons, political thinkers and the Church[5] have generally viewed loyalties and identities based on common descent, history, culture, and language as necessary and good as long as they are limited by higher principles. That is also why ordinary people, including many who are attached to the Church but not paid to be Catholic, are sympathetic to nationalism. They accept loyalty as a virtue, are more concerned with their neighbor than with someone on the other side of the world, and see some form of nationalism as an obvious defense against unmitigated rule by bureaucrats and billionaires. Today's nationalism is basically defensive. Third World nationalism gave form to the desire for independence from colonial powers. In our time nationalism is making a comeback in the West for similar reasons, as a defense against globalism. That is why today's French and German nationalists oppose big business and Eurocrats but not each other. Their nationalism is not a struggle against local autonomy or the Church. Nor is it a matter of national competition or suppression of minorities. Instead, it is a way of protecting local identities and networks of solidarity from disruption by a global commercial and bureaucratic order.

It is the ruling classes and not (as Marx and Engels thought) "the working men" who have no country. The latter are infinitely distant from transnational elites, and their primary attachments will always be local and particular. Money, power, and deals can be pursued anywhere, so people at the top—kings, aristocrats, top bureaucrats, wealthy businessmen—always tend to be cosmopolitan. Educational, scholarly, and media organizations also tend in that direction, since they aim at mastery through universal principles, and in any case mostly align themselves with money and power. That is why nationalism is seen as an irrational and implicitly violent populist threat to social and political order. Our rulers cannot control it, and they do not understand it, or much else about those they rule, whose lives are infinitely distant from their own. So it arouses in them the same feelings of rage and fear that communism did in the nineteenth century.

---

5 See, for example, Pope Pius XI, *Mit Brennender Sorge*.

## Cosmopolitanism

The liberal and globalist dream of a universal rational system based solely on economics, human rights, and regulatory bureaucracy is vain. Inherited religious and cultural connections and identities preceded global enterprises and transnational bureaucracies, and they will outlast them, because they are necessary for a decent and functional life.

Social life is a system of networks. The shape of the world to come depends on what form these networks take. The ones that attract the most loyalty will either be local and regional, as they mostly have been in Europe, where demographic stability has allowed complex local and regional networks of cooperation to develop, or they will be based on non-local and somewhat inward-turning communities like clans, castes, religious sects, and national diasporas, as has been common in places like the Middle East and Central and South Asia that have long been subject to disruptive invasions.

Reliance on local networks and identities has important political benefits. States and governments govern particular territories. If the social networks by which people live are mostly local and territorial, then government can be closely tied to society. The people of every village, town, and region, and of the country as a whole, can see themselves as a people with interests, understandings, and ways that are sufficiently distinct and coherent to guide their government and make it their own. The outcome is symbolized by the contrast between the traditional European city, with its cathedral, city hall, and charter of local privileges, and the traditional Levantine city, with its governor appointed by the sultan (in essence a military dictator) and its walled quarters inhabited by separate national and religious groups. In the former, government of, by, and for the people can be more than an empty phrase. This was the hope behind Brexit and the Trump movement.

Historically, in America we have been able to continue the European approach in spite of sporadic large-scale immigration. We did so with the aid of an emphasis on local government, civic participation, independent families, and local church communities that was inherited from the original English settlers and furthered by an emphasis on patriotism and the assimilation of immigrants, who in the past mostly came from the European cultural sphere. But the European and American approach is now in decline. Among well-placed people, attachment to local connections is considered alarmingly retrogressive. Instead, we are expected to rise above parochial identities and live by our connections to people all over the world. With that in mind, constant mass immigration from everywhere, without any attempt at the cultural assimilation that is now viewed as racist, is considered a moral imperative, because it breaks up the bigotries of localism. That may work for the people at the top, but it does not for people in general. For them, something less universal and less featureless is needed.

Even so, there are difficulties with any attempt to find a continuing place for nationalism. What can it mean in an ever more diverse and ever more technologically oriented country of 330 million, especially in an age in which electronics and cheap transportation annihilate distance? People complain that conservatism has neither conserved anything nor known what it should conserve. The same may turn out to be true for nationalism. A national tradition includes a great many things, and without something higher toward which it is oriented—which is now lacking—it might be thought to point almost anywhere. The actual development of America and Western tradition has led to the situation in which we now find ourselves, in which they are thought to stand for openness to everything from everywhere. If so, how can it help us focus our lives today or in the foreseeable future?

Behind the need for particular community and local identity is the need for even more basic changes that allow such communities and identities to exist, function, and respond to new situations while remaining coherent. Some such changes are inevitable, since life must go on and people will not long tolerate the intolerable, but they may well arrive through the decline of existing communities and the growth of new and perhaps cruder but more coherent ones. Most likely, disintegration of today's communities and the walls that protect them will continue. As that happens, neither Americanism, universal ideals, and the heritage of Western Civilization on the one hand nor ethnic nationalism on the other will have the substance needed to replace them. Instead, society will fragment into groupings and networks that are small and coherent enough to be functional, based on primordial connections and identities that reconstitute themselves when disrupted. Public life as understood in the West will disappear.

Without a fundamental change of direction, then, the future is likely to tend toward mafia-ridden tribalism overseen by corrupt public authorities and their wealthy cronies. Community and identity are not going away, because people live by them and always reconstruct them when they are lost. The only issue is whether they will be civilized or barbaric. It will be difficult to keep them civilized in the world growing up around us, and the current attempt to extirpate them is making it impossible.

# 15

# Tradition

Appealing to natural law and particular community is a helpful beginning, but abstract conceptions must be brought down to earth and embodied in the culture and practices of particular communities to be useful. In particular, natural law needs tradition to make it concrete, decide its implications, and tell us how to put it into effect. And community needs an authoritative tradition to exist at all. But in our time tradition has lost authority, so it has become difficult to appeal to it publicly. Since that is so, it will be useful to make explicit how it works and why it is needed.

## What tradition is

General principles leave a great deal open. Biology tells us not to eat dirt, natural law tells us not to eat other people, the science of nutrition give us advice about types and quantities of food, and human sociability tells us it is good to prepare food well, eat it with others, and show politeness while with them. But beyond such universals, eating is a human activity that reflects a variety of personal, cultural, and aesthetic considerations. Whether someone eats horse flesh or frog legs is likely to depend on the custom of his community, but personal taste also enters into the matter.

Similar principles apply to other areas of conduct. It is natural for a community to have sexual standards that restrain desire. In many respects these standards are broadly similar across societies because they are based fairly directly on natural human tendencies. Thus, incest and adultery are quite generally forbidden. But details vary: is it acceptable to marry a first cousin? How bad are sexual relations outside marriage, and what do you do about them? How should a community deal with courtship and matchmaking? And how about standards of decency in speech and dress? Social life requires answers to such questions, and they get answered somehow even though judgments may differ and theoretical arguments continue. Circumstances force decision, and concrete decisions imply general principles. So somehow or other an orthodoxy and specific system of conduct is instituted. As demonstrated by the "Me Too" movement, and by heightened concern about sexual contact between young and old, that principle applies to our society like all others. There is no such thing as sexual freedom.

This process of answering specific questions leads to the development of tradition. Since what becomes traditional is normally what has worked for people, tradition allows successful accidents, half-understood implications, and a huge variety of experiences to accumulate and take concrete form in symbols, practices, and beliefs that put the patterns of a good life in usable form. That process can go astray, since people never do anything perfectly, but it ensures that whatever social orthodoxy emerges is more likely to be functional and within the bounds of reason than the speculations of supposed experts.

## Authority

In an age of checklists, decision trees, and zero tolerance, accepting tradition is a puzzling notion. People think of it as mindless habit based on chance, old beliefs, or the demands of the powerful. Accepting it, they believe, means giving up on reason, doing what has always been done no matter what, or accepting an external rule that has nothing to do with the situation actually at hand. What else could it mean, they ask, when every situation is different, each of us has his own thoughts and goals, reason is a matter of studies and statistics, and social authority means either submitting to someone else's demands or following rules we have agreed to for our own purposes? That is the liberal concept of man as autonomous, society as contract and mechanism, and knowledge as neutral, impersonal, and progressive.

In fact, though, accepting tradition is simply acting as a human being. Our actions are not isolated from each other. They reflect a system of habits and understandings that is both individual—each of us develops his own way of doing things—and social. So

## Tradition

our habits and understandings are our own, but not simply our own. We pick them up from others, and when people live by a system of habits and understandings, work out the bugs, find it satisfactory, and call it good, it becomes the tradition of the community.

Accepting tradition, and indeed membership in a particular society, includes accepting the understandings of identity that are part of that tradition and society. Social identity gives you a position in a system of loyalties, customs, and relationships. To take a tradition seriously is to take that system and position seriously and view it as basic to your way of life and who you are. For example, the United States government and its legal order have been basic to our way of life in America. So Americans have usually taken them to heart when saying, "I am American," viewing them as part of what they are. In contrast, an Afghan may not view citizenship as basic to his identity, since he may not care about national governments or boundaries. The former keep changing, and his important ties are to his village, clan, and relatives, who may live on both sides of a border. So why should he feel special loyalty to the people who have most recently taken power in Kabul and the regions over which they claim authority?

Like other people, though, he will accept some tradition and the identities that are part of it. This human practice of course brings in all the difficulties of accepting authority of any sort: it is sometimes wrong, different authorities tell us different things, and so on. Nonetheless, we accept authority, including that of tradition, because we are social, and social life and indeed an orderly life in accordance with reason requires it. There are sometimes bad or misleading traditions, but the same applies to all authorities, and we cannot do without them.

## Paradox of traditionalism

Current ways of thinking reject the authority of tradition, and that puts those who accept it in an odd position. Traditionalists today must appeal to history while opposing its direction, promote authority by denying what recognized authorities tell us, and exalt natural growth while denouncing what has actually grown up in the West over the past several hundred years.

Tradition, like culture, is normally the unspoken background to all we say and do. So it is evident that something has gone wrong when its adherents turn argumentative and become traditionalist. But we must deal with the situation in which we find ourselves. That situation is defined not by tradition as such, which is always basic to human life, but by its disruption through the attempt to base it entirely on liberal principles like consent and the maximization of liberty, equality, and wealth. This attempt cannot succeed and indeed contradicts itself.

Liberalism is a tradition that refuses to recognize its nature as such, and depends for its functioning on non-liberal traditions that in principle it opposes. In spite of its aspiration toward transparent rationality, it cannot work without the traditional understandings and relationships that it despises, and the customs of the ordinary people whom it insults. For example, actual systems of law rely on loyalties and understandings that are not altogether liberal, like a belief in the majesty of the law and the obedience that belief inspires. Also, those merely subject to the law are obviously not equal to those who decide and enforce it. Such circumstances mean that liberal society will always, by its own standards, be radically flawed. As liberalism develops, so does its opposition to traditional arrangements. The result is that the development of liberalism gradually destroys the social order needed for it to exist. Recent proposals to abolish the police and teach schoolchildren that their country is fundamentally evil are its natural outcome.

More broadly, the attempts to eradicate "racism," "sexism," "homophobia," and the like, which are defined ever more loosely, are in substance attempts to destroy normal human ties—those consisting of obligations to particular people based on specific affiliations such as family, inherited community, and religion—and replace them with abstract commercial and bureaucratic arrangements considered more just and rational. But contract, bureaucracy, and abstract altruism simply do not have the force of concrete obligations to family, friends, and actual communities. The attempt to rationalize social life therefore weakens the public sense of mutual obligation, leading to social isolation and ill-feeling, and to soaring crime rates, psychological disorders, and welfare costs. It also destroys any basis for the self-sacrificing loyalty that is necessary for a society to survive and function. Why sacrifice your interests unless refusal to do so would betray who you are? If you have a position of power, why not use it for your benefit and that of your family and friends? A public-spirited elite is unlikely to survive in a diverse multicultural society in which there are few common loyalties and ever less social trust, and in which many of the elite view themselves as entitled recipients of compensation for claimed oppression rather than disinterested providers of benefits and protections to others.

The liberal state cannot recognize the source of such ills—the liberal understanding of man as an individual utility-maximizer—without destroying the basis of its legitimacy. So these ills remain unremedied, grow worse, and in the end destroy it. In the meantime, the liberal state's growing disconnection from reality corrupts political thought and language, resulting in the intolerant absurdities of wokeness.

## Objections

Its paradoxical nature makes it easy to object to traditionalism. One objection is that it is meaningless, since everything people do is part of a tradition. After all, we all have some idea of what things are, what they amount to, and how to deal with them, and do not usually make those ideas up ourselves. On the whole, we have them because that is the way the people with whom we are at home look at things, and because the whole system of understandings we have picked up from others works and we are attached to it and them. So praising tradition, someone might say, tells us nothing about what anyone should do or think. There is Catholic tradition, Mafia tradition, Buddhist tradition, Bolshevik tradition, anarchist tradition, and so on. Each of them is complex, as complex as the people involved and the situations they deal with. And in a Catholic society there are likely to be traditions of devotion, orthodoxy, and rigor, but also of laxness, skepticism, heresy, atheism, and criminality. And every tradition develops, that is its genius, so an apparent break in any of them can always be seen as a new development that is likely a natural response to changed circumstances and deeper insight.

Under such circumstances, someone might ask, why pick out some tendency or stage within a community's overall tradition and call that the tradition of the community to the exclusion of all others? Are other aspects and developments of the tradition irrelevant to the whole?

And then there is the practical problem of how people live today. Tradition exists within networks of specific human relations: the life of a village, or a particular region, social class, nation, or religion. Today mobility and communications make such things much harder to define. We deal with most of life through impersonal commercial and bureaucratic structures, and through electronic networks that bathe us in commercial pop culture and connect us immediately to everyone everywhere. So tradition, as an overall way of understanding life and establishing patterns for living, loses its natural setting, falls into disuse, and gives way to image, impulse, fashion, profit, legal compulsion, reliance on real or claimed expertise, and the arts of persuasion and deception.

Such objections seem more impressive than they are. Some of them simply note that tradition is subject to confusion and disruption. That is true, especially today, but it says nothing about its human function and necessity. If coherent traditions are necessary, then conditions that destroy them will not last, however strong the forces behind them. Others ignore the nature of tradition as a human activity that can be carried on well or badly. We cannot live without habit, but some of our habits are bad. Similarly, the necessity of tradition does not mean it can never go wrong. For example, a tradition that aspires primarily to radical choice, change, and self-sufficiency makes no sense because it denies the aspects of human life—the need for continuity and for the slow accumulation of experience, practices, and symbols through the events of many lives—that give tradition its value and authority in the first place. So it is an incoherent tradition that is not worth following, with no more relation to a healthy one than a riot has to a town meeting.

Many objections arise from a superficial and literal-minded view of what tradition is. It is not simply a list of dos and do-nots or register of what particular groups of people have done repeatedly. It points beyond itself to a patterned vision of human goods, and ultimately the good life, that cannot be adequately known or realized without its aid. Thus, musical tradition has to do with melody, rhythm, and harmony, and beyond them with beauty and joy. You become a good musician by learning a particular tradition of music. If you lack talent and play badly, or lack honesty and steal your teacher's violin, that does not become part of the musical tradition, even if you inspire similar conduct in others, because it does not advance the goods with which the tradition is concerned. Similar observations hold elsewhere. Religious tradition has to do with coming closer to God, and an overall tradition of life has to do with the good life in general. Tendencies at odds with these goals may coexist with the traditions, but they are not part of it.

## Development

Man is traditional, but not only traditional. He is also rational, so that he acts in accordance with principles and ideals. These are most often implicit as the grammar of a language is implicit, but they are nonetheless real. As he learns to apply them he comes to understand them better, and develops habits and understandings that may become part of his tradition because they help achieve its goals. Tradition and principles are thus intertwined. Each supports and affects the other.

## Growth

Tradition is always about something that transcends it. So it can be improved upon, and a healthy tradition accommodates changes that better realize its goals. Such changes most often escape notice except in retrospect, since they usually result from a gradual change of emphasis as some aspects of the tradition get called on more and others less, and from practices and formulations that originally looked like minor variations but become more than that as they accumulate. Examples within Catholic tradition include the development of rituals and devotions, and the development of doctrine as understood by Saint John Henry Newman.

Also, tradition can visibly need reform. Like individual character, it can include bad habits and understandings as well as good ones. The good are more important, since we cannot live a human life outside a social tradition, but the bad usually attract more attention because they cause more problems. When imperfections in a tradition become troublesome, people normally respond by reinforcing the understandings and practices that seem most important, and abandoning or changing less important ones that seem to interfere with the basic goods with which the tradition is concerned. Some parts of the tradition are always more important than others, and there is always some flexibility in how to reconcile purpose and practice. Very often the response includes going back to the sources: how can we become more like our great predecessors?

Religious reformers provide an example. They complain about current practices but most often do so in the name of older and more fundamental traditions and the goods to which they point. They appeal from the Pharisees to Moses and the prophets, or from current practices in a monastery to the example of its founder. And they show how even false traditions point toward something better. Justin Martyr saw the seeds of the *Logos* in Greek tradition, and in our own time Pope Benedict XVI annoyed some people by noting that "Christ was the savior for whom [the American Indians] were silently longing,"[1] a longing that was imprinted in certain aspects of their traditions.

An intelligent and internally consistent tradition that understands its own limits and purpose will thus include at least implicitly a principle of self-criticism. Today, for example, there is a tradition of elevator music within the larger tradition of Western music. Those who carry on the former most often recognize what they are doing as a decline from the latter, and would rather pursue things that the larger tradition recognizes as better.

## Decline

Sometimes moderate reform seems insufficient. Changes in circumstances or developments in the tradition itself may bring out

---

[1] Pope Benedict XVI, Apostolic Journey to Brazil: Inaugural Session of the Fifth General Conference of the Bishops of Latin America and the Caribbean at the Conference Hall of the Shrine of Aparecida (May 13, 2007).

## Tradition

basic flaws that eventually become crippling and destroy the goods for which it was established. When the flaws resist remedy, the result can be a crisis of the tradition and even of general public order. Eventually tradition and equilibrium will reestablish themselves, but there is no telling how long that will take or how good the results will be.

The thought of classical antiquity had no way to resolve the questions arising within it, so it ended in skepticism, superstition, and unmoored mysticism. And in China the ruling classes were eventually forced to recognize that their traditional ways did not enable them to compete with the industrialized world and its gunboats. The Greeks and Romans eventually adopted a new system—Christianity—that overcame the problems of classical thought and led to an even greater civilization. The Chinese have made progress materially but do not yet seem to have regained their footing as a civilization, a process that can be expected to take a great deal of time and effort.

Our problems today seem equally radical. Changes in popular culture that are obvious to everyone, documented in recent accounts of working-class life like those by Charles Murray[2] and Theodore Dalrymple,[3] make it evident that over the past five or six decades there has been a catastrophic decline in the way of life of old-line non-elite Americans and Englishmen. Recent changes therefore represent a radical deterioration of cultural tradition. That judgment is not a matter of taste: even something as brutally objective as death rates shows that something has gone wrong in how people live.[4] Even so, no one in authority has any intention of dealing with the fundamental problems or even any idea of what they are or what might be done about them. How could they? The elites responsible for dealing with such issues have grown anti-traditional. They are not dissatisfied with this tradition or that, or at a loss how to achieve old goals in new set-

---

2 Murray, *Coming Apart*.
3 Dalrymple, *Life at the Bottom*.
4 Kolata and Tavernise, "It's Not Just Poor White People Driving a Decline in Life Expectancy."

tings. Instead, they want to reject tradition as such and the goods it proposes. That is the meaning of the liberal claim to universal rationality and the growing emphasis on "diversity" and related ideals. And that is the project that leads to the state of social disconnection whose consequences Murray and Dalrymple describe, and has led elites to turn more and more overtly against their own people as inadequate to their vision. Basic tendencies are thus causing basic problems with no end in sight.

Some would describe that as a collapse of the Western tradition. It seems better to describe it as disruption of the tradition by aspects of it, like its emphasis on technology, that have become too dominant. We cannot get by without a tradition; the tradition of the West is the one we have, and there is no superior one available, so we must maintain our loyalty to it and do what we can to bring it back into balance. That project might be successful. "The West" is simply Catholic Christendom 500 years after the Protestant revolt, and it possesses resources that go far beyond the technocratic aspects now dominant. And the technocratic West could not survive without the residual presence of its predecessor, which retains most people's loyalty to some degree and holds the primary loyalty of an increasingly active, self-conscious, and intellectually confident minority. So the materials are there, although the future, as always, is uncertain.

### American tradition

American conservatism provides an example of the difficulties encountered by tradition in the modern world. At bottom, conservatism is the desire to remain true to type. So American conservatism is the desire for America to remain American. That preference is entirely normal. America is a particular human society and as such gives its people a world to live in. We are social beings, and it provides us with a network of connections and gives our lives a certain form and focus. For that reason, it affects us at a very basic level: we are Americans and it would be hard to change that. The result is that it is natural for us to want our country to keep going and remain the sort of place we are used to. It is part of us, and we want that part to be alive and healthy. At least, that is true for many of us.

## Tradition

So loyalty to America is natural for Americans. But what exactly is involved in it? It is difficult to say without saying what America is and what we are as Americans. But questions regarding American identity do not seem to have a good answer. One traditional answer would have been that America is the land of the American people, a particular people whose members were easily recognizable as such by foreigners. The original English settlers and their descendants set the type, with regional variations. Immigrants assimilated to that type, although they contributed something of their own, and some differences—notably, religious differences—hung on as they slowly accommodated themselves to their new environment.

Times change. Mass immigration from all over the world, combined with the new emphasis on racial equality, idealization of "diversity," and ease of travel and communication, have made it ever harder to define who the American people are. And in any case, ethnic nationalism is now roundly denounced as racist, and appeals to specifically American traditions, such as the English basis of our legal system, more and more receive the same treatment. Under such circumstances some other definition of America seems needed. That is why we are now told that America is defined by its commitment to freedom and equality. Or that it is a nation of immigrants, the land of opportunity, and the champion of global democracy. People find these claims plausible, and it is true that American nationality has usually been associated with ideals of freedom and equality. But when those ideals are taken as the sole basis of our national life, with no reference whatever to the particular people who hold them, they are at odds with any very definite national identity or tradition. Worse, defining America solely by reference to them has totalitarian implications—if you do not give official principles your supreme loyalty, you do not belong here!

American conservatism thus has serious weaknesses. Our way of life has tended toward mobility, informality, expansiveness, and enterprise. Our ideals have emphasized freedom, equality, and the universal applicability of the American model. Our general philosophy has alternated between pragmatism and New Age. And we have had no memory of Christendom, myth of common blood, or old regime of throne, altar, and sword, only symbols like the Revolution, Constitution, and Statue of Liberty, to which progressives have a better right than traditionalists. Lacking compelling theories and symbols, and undercut by basic features of American life, thought, and history, American conservatism has been hard-put to define or defend itself. It has never been clear what it should conserve, and its survival has depended on the practical success of American institutions and the national habit of avoiding systematic thought. It has most often taken the form of reverence for "the ideals of the Founding Fathers," that is, for liberalism as it stood at the time of the American Founding, and of an attempt to associate American national symbols with the generic Protestant religiosity that was once such a powerful influence in American life.

By suppressing the development of liberalism and tying it at least notionally to something that transcended it, American conservatism minimized its harm. The potential for harm was real. The American state, especially the federal government, has been primarily a contract for material ends. To survive, social tradition has needed arrangements that make habits and attitudes that relate to more complex and higher ends independent of the state, and those arrangements were a prominent feature of the regime established by the Founders. They included federalism, limited government, local democracy, and informal social control through a combination of moralism, non-doctrinal Protestantism, and traditional habits and prejudices.

Conservative intellectuals tried to build on these arrangements a philosophical notion of America as a free, virtuous, and self-governing society. "Free" suggests anti-traditional qualities, "virtuous" necessary limitations, and "self-governing" the proper balance between the two. So conservative intellectuals praised liberty, insisted on the virtue, moderation, and wisdom of the Constitution and the American people, and denounced overly ideological applications of American ideals that threatened the balance of the system. While logically weak, this compromise between liberalism and tradition held up remarkably well in the face of Civil War and Reconstruction, the New Deal, and twentieth-century wars. Both sides gained from it: tradition needed liberalism for legitimacy, and liberalism needed tradition for stability and survival.

In recent decades, this compromise has fallen apart. It could not stand up to developments like demographic diversification, the rise of the consumer society and electronic mass media, and industrialized mass education. Liberal principles came to be understood and applied more and more singlemindedly, until social unity could no longer be based on vaguely Protestant religiosity and the moral authority of those long-dead propertied heteronormative cis white male slave-owners, the Founding Fathers. The result is that America has become a largely ideological state. Conservative resistance could achieve very little. Simple conservatism is a consensus-based position whose adherents are more strongly attached to family, faith, and community than to theory. It wants to be true to type, whatever the established type happens to be, so it eventually conforms to whatever tendencies are dominant. In an ever-radicalizing age like our own it becomes useless. What can it possibly mean when wokeness and a radically anti-particularist conception of social justice have taken over all significant institutions?

# 16
# The Church

Neither pure tradition nor pure natural law is sufficient for social order. A stable society must be based on an understanding of the world that ties them to each other and to the structure of reality, and so gives them objective authority. Without that they can easily get lost in a maze of conflicting interpretations. So tradition and natural law need religion. Religion in turn needs tradition and natural law to interpret what it tells us. As a practical matter the three stand or fall together. Bringing back one requires bringing back all.

## Beyond tradition

To accept tradition is to accept an inherited understanding of the world as true and sustaining. But tradition has evident weaknesses. It is a composite of symbols, practices, and beliefs, the meanings of which are largely unstated and understandings of which may vary. It is also the way of life of a people as it actually exists. As such, it is likely to incorporate conflict, confusion, error, abuse, vagueness, and a great deal that is simply arbitrary. And in a technological age it is likely, like everything else, to become instrumentalized.

Both the weakness of tradition as a human thing and its concern with the inarticulable make it easy for it to lose coherence. Under stress and uncertainty the unspoken faith implicit in it may not be enough to anchor thought and action and give them a stable orientation. Divisive questions can arise that cannot be settled, and the result will be confusion, disruption, and dissolution.

Reasoning can regularize and reconcile the components of a tradition, and defend it against objection. Government and other social authorities can support it, and provide social and political boundaries that give it a stable setting in which to exist. But tradition is how we make sense of the world, so it must be self-sustaining. To tell it what it must be is to destroy it as tradition. So in a diverse and changing world it can survive neither on its own resources nor on resources supplied by something truly external to itself. Instead, it must point by its nature to something beyond itself that motivates it and to which primary loyalty is owed.

## Faith

Faith is basic to human life. Just as institutions and knowledge depend on the complex of memories, understandings, and habits that constitutes tradition, tradition depends on its connection to a larger order of which it is part, to which it responds, and which it does not fully grasp. So we cannot understand tradition as simply a human institution, for example as the habit of making decisions by reference to what has worked and endured. Tradition tells us what we and our world are, and by doing so it comes to us with an authority that goes beyond anything we can fully explain. We cannot help but depend on it, and our confidence implies a faith that it is not random or arbitrary but revelatory, that through it the bits, pieces, and glimmerings that are immediately available to us have grown into attitudes, practices, beliefs, and symbols that show how things really are and make truths available to us that we cannot attain directly.

Our acceptance of tradition and our understanding of the world thus depend on our trust in things that go beyond what we can perceive or demonstrate. That everyday kind of faith is not foreign to reason, because reason depends on it. Reason cannot demonstrate the conditions of its functioning: the validity of first principles, the trustworthiness of perception, the coherence of memory, or the reliability of the linguistic and cultural setting it needs to operate. It must take them on faith, although that faith, like other aspects of our way of understanding the world, must stand up in the long run to experience and to the reasonings it inspires.

## Religion

What kind of faith is needed depends on circumstances. In the comparatively simple societies preceding the rise of cosmopolitan civilization in the Middle East around the first millennium BC, self-regulating intuitions were enough to maintain the stability and coherence of tradition. The order of human affairs could be identified with that of the cosmos, and the world assumed without argument to be as tradition said it was.

New circumstances brought new needs. As society became more complex, communications improved, and political and social relations became more extensive, questions multiplied, all things became debatable, and tradition had to develop additional features to maintain stability and coherence. Those features forced the manner of dealing with the transcendent—with things that precede and condition the everyday, and are authoritative but difficult to identify and discuss—to become more explicit and formal, and so forced tradition to rely overtly on things that are not purely traditional and customary. The most important change was the increasing religious formalization of the aspects of tradition that relate to ultimate questions. Organized religion gives those things a form, structure, and system of authority that makes them able to assert and defend themselves and insist on their irreplaceable role in human life. When human society becomes ever more a collection of specialized and relatively autonomous pursuits, the transcendent must also become a specialty so that it can avoid displacement or absorption by this-worldly interests and activities.

The need for such formalization has varied by time and place. Until recently it was felt less acutely in India and China than in the civilizations that grew out of the world of the Eastern Mediterranean and Middle East. The former are comparatively compact land masses of sub-continental scale, separated from other major civilizations by natural barriers. As a result, cultural cohesion was challenged less than to their west, and in any event was somewhat less important because of the comparatively limited public life. The Chinese emperor could remain the Son of Heaven until 1912, the Confucians could put cultural tradition where the West put philosophy and religion, and "Hinduism" could simply be acceptance of any somewhat mainstream form of Indian religious tradition. In contrast, the Eastern Mediterranean was a crossroads, marketplace, and arena in which arose strict monotheism, philosophical argument aimed at universal truth, and the ideal of scientific rigor. Multiple enduring centers of culture provided for the confrontation of differing understandings of human life and the world. To survive in such a setting, a way of life had to be able to put its case in a much more explicit, focused, and universalizable form.

From the outside, the departure induced by the formalization of religion from the anonymity and informality of tradition can look like a human construction that functions to maintain the coherence and apparent intelligibility of life and the world. From within, however, it can only appear as the result of an intervention from above. For a long time, then, to live a life of reason has been, in the Western world, to accept the authority of some revelation: the alternative has been willfulness or the reign of shifting subjective opinion. Nothing has happened to change that situation. To the contrary, it appears from the spread of Christianity in China and Korea, Christianity and Islam in Africa, and the ersatz gods of ideology everywhere, including an ideologized form of Hinduism in India, that the need for public, systematic, and comprehensive thought that comes to stable and reliable conclusions has spread well beyond the West.[1] The choice is not between faith and reason but among faiths anchored in what is accepted as revelation.

## Christianity

Revelation as a response to an increasingly cosmopolitan, rational, and differentiated social world did not stop with Moses and the prophets. Judaism is valid only for a single people, and its textual basis and consequent legalism deprives it of adaptability. It lacks the comprehensive and flexible rationality needed to support public order in a post-Hellenistic world that encompasses large populations with diverse national and local traditions and

---

[1] Its insular position and unique, tightly woven culture has enabled Japan to remain a holdout.

accepts the advantages of free public life, including free inquiry on a broad range of issues. A tradition that accepts inquiry and free public life must have a way to bring inquiry to a conclusion on crucial points and draw a reliable line between truth and error that could put things decisively on the wrong track. The more cosmopolitan and diverse the society, the more necessary this becomes. The growing nihilism and manipulativeness of modernity results from its lack of such a thing, especially with regard to questions of good and evil.

Neither pure tradition nor pure rationality nor a purely textual revelation is enough to settle all the practical issues that must be settled for life to go on under such circumstances. It is therefore reasonable to have confidence in a social tradition that provides for rational standards and free public life and inquiry in a cosmopolitan setting only if there is an authoritative method of interpreting its fundamental principles. Since human reason and experience are not enough to resolve all such issues, the method must be understood as embodying an intelligence greater than our own, and thus as equivalent to continuing divine guidance.

Truth that cannot be unambiguously formulated has a necessary personal element. Events and propositions can be construed to signify very different things without violating formal criteria, so knowledge depends on personal orientation and commitment. Tradition, the common mind of a community, has a personal aspect. To believe as a member of a community is to put our trust in its common mind, and let ourselves be formed by it. For that belief to be rational, and to maintain our commitment to truth, we must believe that our community of belief has a relationship to ultimate things that makes it capable of knowing them truly. The Christian account of God become man and still present in his Church makes comprehensible, in the most direct and complete way, how a community can have such a quality. Since God is understood as a living presence in the community here and now, it becomes comprehensible that the decision of the community on disputed matters should determine our understanding. The love, loyalty, and trust toward one's community and tradition that is necessary for coherent thought become reasonable.

# The Church

## Catholicism

When a specific question is to be resolved, the mind of the community must be made concrete through a human authority that is its guardian. Where public life is ordered by principles intended to be final, comprehensive, and yet flexible enough to respond to new circumstances, responsibility for construing them normally falls to a hierarchical college appointed for life. The United States federal judiciary provides an example. Such a college is often headed by a panel, like the United States Supreme Court. However, when the system is not a branch of government but must itself govern an independent society, as in the case of the dominant party in a one-party state, it is usually headed by a single man for the sake of unity, personal responsibility, and the possibility of decisive action. If the public principles are to be understood as stable, objectively valid, and independent of human will, the other members of the hierarchical college should retain a certain independent status so that there remains an element of distributed judgment. A traditional European monarchy, with its hereditary nobility, provides an analogy.

The arrangement of belief and authority described is that of the Catholic Church. Only Roman Catholicism, through its hierarchy united by common discipline and doctrine and headed by the pope, is able to speak and act in a way that is personal and authoritative but also collective. Roman Catholicism thus displays, in the most clear and consistent way possible, the natural form for truth to take in a world of free public life. It is altogether in character that Catholicism fostered learning, philosophy, and the arts, that the distinctive institutions of Catholic Christendom have included universities, free political institutions, and modern natural science, and that Western culture was so fecund for so long. The decisive rejection of Christianity—which even in its Protestant and liberalizing forms has depended on the Roman Church and pope for its coherence and force—has been accompanied by irrationalism, radical decline in all aspects of non-technological culture, and the attempt to reduce politics and public life to purely technical functions and so abolish them. *Extra ecclesiam nulla salus:* without the authoritative universal Church headed by the pope, coherent thought with regard to the world as a whole, at least in a cosmopolitan society with Western traditions of public life and rational inquiry, becomes impossible in the long run.

Today, of course, the Church is a mess. Poor leadership, together with internal divisions and defections, deprives her of the practical ability to speak and act in a personal and authoritative way. But that cannot be a strong objection to her authority when authority is necessary and everything else is a greater mess. She has lasted a very long time and survived a great many ups and downs, and in principle she remains what she always has been, so it seems possible even today that she will return to type and become once again capable of joining and ordering a complex of particularities into a civilization.

To say that something looks like what a system of truth should look like does not, of course, prove that it really is a system of truth. And to argue that we in the West today must accept Catholic Christianity if we are to understand ourselves as reasonable is not precisely to prove the truth of Catholic Christianity, but only to argue the impossibility of rejecting it and retaining our sanity. Those who reject Catholic Christianity on grounds of enlightenment should tell us what their alternative is.

But here we get to a paradox. As the book says, seek ye first the kingdom of God and all else will be added unto you (Mt 6:33). God is not a means to an end. We will not escape technocracy and create a better way of life through a "noble lie." Our search for a better world thus ends in the recognition that we will not get that world if we make it our highest goal. Unless the Lord build the house, they labor in vain that build it (Ps 127:1). We must want most of all to live in the truth.

# PART IV
Turning Around

# 17

# A Choice, Not an Echo

A better social order, one that accepts the natural ordering of human life, requires a religion that is up to the task. The problem of responding effectively to the disintegration of human identity has thus turned out to be largely the problem of building up Catholic faith and community. But a religion cannot be adopted just to improve the social order. To be useful, it must be accepted as true. For that reason faithful Catholics can be expected to be at the center of whatever solid progress is made. From this point onward this book will mostly be addressed to such people. Even so, the arguments and discussion will not be based on specifically Catholic beliefs and may be useful to others.

## Individual commitment

The Church and world need a concrete practical response to liberal modernity that offers more hope than passivity, supine accommodation, or retreat into fantasy. But what?

We can only start where we are. During the Warring States period in China (c. 475–221 BC), Confucius thought deeply about the problem of fundamental reform in bad times. How can anything be built when the foundation, materials, and workmen are lacking? He responded:

> The ancients who wished to illustrate illustrious virtue throughout the kingdom first ordered well their own states. Wishing to order well their states, they first regulated their families. Wishing to regulate their families, they first cultivated their persons. Wishing to cultivate their persons, they first rectified their hearts. Wishing to rectify their hearts, they first sought to be sincere in their thoughts. Wishing to

be sincere in their thoughts, they first extended to the utmost their knowledge.[1]

So people need to start at the beginning by conforming their understanding of themselves and the world to reality, and then get their lives in order, beginning with what is closest to them. The effort could begin with things as simple as educating ourselves, clearing our minds of cant, avoiding trashy pop culture, broadening our practical competencies, and learning how to earn a living without lying or servility. With these as a background, we can associate with the like-minded, and start and raise families. Those who do so will at least be able to help themselves and their family and neighbors, and may be able to do much more.

What is important is to get started and keep at it. If you do not do everything, do some things; if you cannot do them perfectly, do them as well as you can; and if you fail, get up and try again. Direction and intention are everything: that is what G. K. Chesterton meant when he said that if a thing is worth doing, it is worth doing badly. Above all, though, we should aspire to a standard of truth and loyalty beyond practical considerations. We cannot force or fake our way to a better life. If we want the world to be more Catholic, we must be Catholic ourselves.

## Difficulties

A feature of today's public life that makes progress impossible is the narrowness of public discussion. Only a small range of views are allowed, and these ignore basic human realities. That is the situation that makes political correctness possible, and has led, for example, to the rapid rise of transgenderism. Another problem is that politics today has to do with control of government policy—passing laws, funding programs, and so on—and thus the use of regulation and bureaucracy to achieve defined goals. How can that help if the problem is technocracy? To deal with these difficulties Catholics need to expand the range of discussion, broaden the public understanding of political life, and

---

[1] Confucius, *The Great Learning*.

emphasize the limits on what purely political interventions can do. People need to recognize the importance of things that come before politics, like religion, culture, and human nature, and respect their integrity. If they can be brought to do so, politics in the modern sense—the effort to subject the world to man's will—will become less imperialistic.

Catholics will not broaden political discussion by concentrating on "what brings us together." Secular progressives are intransigent because they deny the reality of anything that does not fit into their narrow view of the world. If non-progressives put social unity first, they will always give way to the secular progressives. Doing so defines today's respectable opposition—otherwise it would not be respectable. The result, of course, is that progressives always win. Compare the response to the Black Lives Matter riots in the summer of 2020 and the pro-Trump riot on January 6, 2021: when the grievances were progressive the response was general non-prosecution and doing what the rioters wanted. When they were non-progressive, the answer was to crush all opposition through military occupation and draconian punishments.

Our response to the current situation must be to chart our own course based on what is real and important. The truth about man and the world must come first. That idea alarms people, because they view fixed truths as intolerant. To the contrary, however, it sets us free: if truth is put first, principles such as freedom, equality, human nature, and the human good can be seen from a perspective that gives each its due without one tyrannizing the others. Our standard should therefore be clarity and integrity rather than respectability or immediate effectiveness. If we present something coherent and cogent, we have a chance in the long run. If we try to make ourselves acceptable to the *New York Times*, we have none at all.

## The power of example

To achieve anything, we have to find once again our own way of speaking, use it publicly until people get used to it, and make arguments that go beyond the principles of freedom, equality, utility, and tolerance that now rule public discussion. In particular, we need to bring human nature and substantive public goods back into the conversation. The project is complex, because the technocratic outlook makes it difficult for people today to understand such things, and in so far as they begin to understand them, they have no idea what to do about them. Suppose, for example, someone comes to agree that the traditional family is best. Does that mean a National Family Board should be created to issue regulations on who does the dishes and takes out the trash?

Clearly not, but the technocratic assumptions that pervade public discussion make it difficult to understand what else could be done. We can challenge those assumptions, but that makes the argument too complex and abstract to make much headway. To cut through these difficulties we need not only to present the Catholic view but to demonstrate it in practice, so people can see what it is, how it works, and how it can change lives. That would illustrate the practical benefits of authoritative cultural community and natural law views on sexual restraint and complementarity, so they could be taken more seriously in public discussion, and the idea eventually take hold that law and social institutions should accept them and foster their adoption in daily life. The attempt is obviously worth the effort. Even if it fails politically, demonstrating the Catholic view in practice would give us a better way of life and benefit those around us. Indeed, to say we should demonstrate it to persuade others is obviously backwards: we should live more like Catholics because it is best to do so, with persuading others as a side-benefit. Even so, a consciousness that others are watching can help people act better. Many parents, for instance, have straightened out their lives when they have had children to raise.

When we can show a way of life that others have reason to aspire to, and are truly ready at all times to give everyone who asks "a reason for that hope which is in us" (1 Pt 3:15), we will be better able to engage with others effectively. This is by far the greatest social contribution we can make as Catholics. A defense of marriage and family, for example, would involve first and foremost the laity getting their lives in order. Those most directly involved—fathers and mothers, husbands and wives, young people looking to found a family—should take the lead. A genuinely pastoral clergy would support their efforts with clear and forthright teaching and an emphasis on communicating Catholic moral understandings to a world that has lost touch with natural law and thus human reality. The clergy should also set an example of adherence to Catholic moral teaching in their own lives. In an age of *Amoris Laetitia*, James Martin's *Building a Bridge*, loose morals in the clergy, the German "Synodal Way," and widespread assimilation at all levels of the Church to the attitudes and way of life of those around us, it is painfully obvious how much needs to be done.

The emphasis on clarity and integrity should also inform Catholic charitable involvement. We need to love our neighbor, but in a way that respects natural law and the total human good. This will often require us to do it our own way rather than by joining some secular effort, such as a push for social welfare legislation, that will often be based on a technocratic understanding of human life. The direct assistance to individuals Dorothy Day and many other Catholics have given can perhaps provide a model. So we need to stand ready to put our own efforts and resources into the effort, and—as always—to be as wise as serpents.

As an example, considerations of economic rationality and consumer choice are turning healthcare into a system for managing human resources—maintaining those that are useful, scrapping those that are not[2]—and providing customers with biotechnological consumer "goods" like babies, abortions, and sex-change operations. Layered onto these goals is a growing aversion to taking any risks at all with respect to health in many situations. This last tendency seems attributable to the hedonistic and strictly this-worldly outlook now in vogue, together with the technocratic drive toward absolute control of all things. A recent result of it is that those dying from COVID-19 were very often left to die alone, deprived of family and the sacraments, because precautions against contagion might possibly fail. It is important to argue against such understandings of healthcare, but even

---

[2] See Kelly Malone, "Medically Assisted Deaths Could Save Millions in Health Care Spending: Report."

more important to display opposing understandings in action. The legal environment is making it difficult for professionals to do that by practicing medicine in a way that respects natural law. But we can always do something: Mother Teresa provides one model, and there are others. The conduct of the hierarchy during the recent pandemic, and the willingness of many Catholic institutions to cooperate with breaches of the natural law, show how far we have to go.

## Dangers of assimilation

To give people a vision by which they can orient themselves, we need to present something more than the work of particular individuals and organizations; we need to propose a better way of life for the whole community. What is needed and how do we get there?

A minimalist answer is to take what comes and trust in Providence. So forget grand strategy, this approach tells us, overall plans are useless. Even when times seem bad, every situation is an opportunity for each of us to live out the Gospel; all things work together for good for those who love God.[3] If a variety of people direct their efforts in the right direction, those efforts will eventually come together, since good supports good, and a better way of life for the whole people will emerge. Ideas are rightly judged by their consequences, so if we act on good ones they will ultimately win out.

There is a great deal of sense to this: the kingdom of God cometh not with observation, and it certainly comes not with planning. We cannot predict the future, so we must take what comes, deal with it as best we can, and let God look to ultimate results. This is inevitably a large part of how the Church deals with all circumstances in which she finds herself. But it cannot be the whole story. Man is a social being, and it is hard for him to live a good life by himself. He is also a rational being, and prudence is a Christian virtue. The Church believes in pastoral prudence, so she does what she can to promote favorable settings for

---

3 Rom. 8:28.

the Christian life. This involves examining basic features of life today and asking what is needed to provide a better life for the Catholic community.

To the extent the pastors of the Church fail to do that, the laity will have to do what they can. Some points seem obvious. Lack of continuity has routinely disabled attempts to hamper liberal modernity. Such efforts require continuity of effort, but liberal modernity divides and weakens human connections. It is dispiriting to read the American Catholic journalist Carol Jackson Robinson's accounts of Catholic Action seventy years ago.[4] So much dedication and effort, so much hope, and where has it all gone? Like many others she hoped for great things from the Second Vatican Council, but was cruelly disappointed.

As things are, the formal institutions through which education, employment, and public discussion are carried on take Catholics out of Catholic settings. That makes it harder for them to cooperate for common goals. Worse, it puts them in settings committed to anti-Catholic understandings. Increasingly, for example, large institutions insist on celebration of every religion, way of life, and purported family form and conception of identity as equivalent to every other. Activities not carried on through large institutions are mostly carried on through electronic media that dominate leisure time, shape our relations to our fellows, disintegrate the close social networks that define who we are, and encourage people to follow individual choice and taste wherever they may lead—as long as where they lead is "tolerant." The result is an environment and way of life that promotes hedonistic careerism as a rational, tolerant, and socially beneficial outlook on life.

If we are immersed in that setting, most of us will get swamped and go where the current carries us. If Catholics go home from Mass and spend the rest of the week awash in pop culture and official propaganda in settings that trivialize religious concerns, enforce perverse conceptions of right, wrong, human nature, and the good life, and have no connection to Catholic identity, the strong will no doubt survive. But not all of us are

---

4 Carol Jackson Robinson, *The Perverse Generation*.

strong, and the Church cannot leave her members to sink or swim.[5]

## Distinctiveness

We try to avoid occasions of sin, so if a situation threatens faith and morals we should look for ways to avoid it. Catholics need to extricate themselves from the bad influences in which they are entangled. It follows that most of us need a certain degree of separation from what mainstream society has become to find connections that sustain us. To that end, the Church needs to emphasize her nature as a complex of local communities.

Love of God means a focus on faith, prayer, worship, and right conduct, and thus on the communities in which such things are fostered and become habitual. Love of neighbor involves enabling our neighbor to live more easily a life in accordance with nature, reason, and ultimately the love of God. To that end the Faith must become incarnate in all the complexities of human life and make them her own. For that to happen, the Church needs her own tradition and culture. But tradition and culture are always particular, tied to particular communities, histories, and identities, and thus to the boundaries that define and guard them. To promote specifically Catholic tradition and culture, then, we must break with common ways of doing things and establish our own forms of life together in which Catholics can carry on Christian lives. If we merge into the increasingly featureless society that surrounds us, we too will become featureless and unable to benefit ourselves or others.

## Benedict of Nursia

What specifically should be done? There is certainly no universal answer, but a name that often comes to mind in this connection is Benedict of Nursia. Benedict himself had one very definite way;[6] others, notably Rod Dreher in a bestselling book,[7]

---

[5] Not everyone thinks the Church of the future will be able to accommodate weaklings. See, e.g., Romano Guardini, *The End of the Modern World*.

[6] Benedict of Nursia, *The Rule of St. Benedict*.

[7] *The Benedict Option: A Strategy for Christians in a Post-Christian Nation*.

have presented ways loosely based on his but much less well defined.

Benedict himself wanted to break worldly ties so he could follow Christ and grow closer to God. To that end he went to the mountains to live away from distractions, and eventually established a rule whereby those who were doing likewise could live together productively, with each helping the others toward their common goal. He did not, of course, originate such efforts. Christian monasticism had begun centuries before, notably in the deserts of Egypt. And before that, in the Bible, God had repeatedly called people out of established ways of life to something separate, as when he called Abraham out of Ur and Moses out of Egypt. Such transformations were often marked by a change of name and the foundation of a new people.

Jesus likewise called his disciples to leave home, family, and possessions to follow him. By baptism they would be reborn as new men and women and form a new Christian people. An aspiration to break worldly ties for the sake of a transformation of life and identity is thus part of Christianity. Christians are Christian within the Church, the Church aspires to be holy, and the Bible notes a resulting need for separation that is sometimes expressed quite sharply:

> Know you not that the friendship of this world is the enemy of God? (Jas 4:4)
>
> Do not love the world or the things of the world. If anyone loves the world, the love of the Father is not in him. (1 Jn 2:15–17)
>
> Bear not the yoke with unbelievers.... Go out from among them, and be ye separate, saith the Lord, and touch not the unclean thing. (2 Cor 6:14–17)

Such injunctions cannot be taken categorically, since grace does not abolish natural connections. Paul enjoined converts to maintain close family ties,[8] Jesus insisted we should honor our

---

8  1 Cor 7:14.

father and mother,[9] and the examples of the Good Samaritan and woman of Canaan shows that the neighbor with whom we concern ourselves need not be of the same religious community. Even so, experience had taught Benedict to take them seriously. Nor did he lack models. As mentioned, there had long been solitaries and groups pursuing, in a more or less organized way, a secluded life of prayer, abstinence, and penitence. Benedict wanted to follow in their footsteps, and his famous Rule for doing so in community developed previous schemes of monastic life into a system that proved enduringly useful. That system included the lifetime vows of stability, obedience, and perpetual conversion that defined the life of a Benedictine monk and made him part of a particular community and so defined who he was as a monk.

## Variants

Such is the "Benedict Option" of Benedict of Nursia. But most current discussion relates to a "Benedict Option" understood in a highly figurative sense, as an approach to the Christian life that allows family life, ordinary occupations, and other everyday connections, activities, and identities to continue while holding mainstream secular life at something of a distance. The two are, of course, quite different, and the latter is much more broadly defined, but there is a family resemblance. Both have to do with closeness to God and a better way of life in a community that attempts to turn away from the distractions and corruptions of the world.

The Church has always supported some degree of separation. In most respects, the early Christians lived as other people did. They interacted with them in their daily lives, thought of themselves as (for instance) Romans, prayed for the emperor, accepted Roman authority within the limits of divine law, and sometimes held positions in the army and government. Even so, they carried on a way of life different enough and superior enough to that led by others to transform the Roman world, and maintaining that way of life required some separation. For example, it meant

9 Mk 7:9–13; 10:8.

refraining from any semblance of participation in pagan worship. Since many social observances, such as popular festivals, were associated with pagan worship, that was a broad prohibition. Christians also felt obliged to avoid many of the popular entertainments of the time: the theater, chariot races, gladiatorial contests. And then, of course, they met regularly for worship and fellowship, and preferentially married each other.

Separation was needed even though mainstream public life was much less intrusive then than now. It was a world of peasants, artisans, small shopkeepers, face-to-face relationships, and education mainly at home, or otherwise locally and privately. The religious unity of the ancient city had long been lost, the state mostly stayed out of everyday affairs, and the Roman games and doings of temple prostitutes were not livestreamed everywhere. So life centered much more on the household and on informal local communities, where Catholic understandings could carry weight even when Catholic numbers were low overall. The great cities of the Empire, where Christianity first established itself, included a variety of communities, each living in its own way. The Christians could simply form one more, and they did.

## How it grows

There is nothing unusual about the Church as a complex of distinct and cohesive local communities. Such communities arise with regard to almost any distinct way of life. A way of life grows out of an understanding of what matters and how the world is, and people naturally try to promote cooperation and reduce disputes and misunderstandings by associating with those who share such things. People with similar interests form clubs. Scholars join together in colleges and universities. A large city is likely to have Chinese and hipster neighborhoods. And the British and American press ran a number of sympathetic pieces a few years ago on the plight of people who found they had neighbors who voted for Trump[10] or Brexit.[11] Some were thinking of moving elsewhere.

---

10  Michael Kruse, "What Do You Do If a Red State Moves to You?"
11  Karl Whitney, "Why Andy Martin, Documenter of a Changing Sunderland, Has Left His City."

So it is entirely natural for religious groups to set themselves off in some way, initially without special effort or intention. People pursue what they like and avoid what they do not. They think the schools are bad, and look for something better for their children. They do not like the spectacles in the Colosseum or on TV, so they go square-dancing instead. As they do those things, they naturally link up with like-minded people. If they like anything at all, they may join a fan club. If they see a common key to getting their lives together, they form a support group. The more humanly important the object of their interest, the more such choices come to determine their network of social connections, other activities, overall way of life, and self-understanding.

As time passes, standards and boundaries develop that mark such people off as a separate community. They become aware of themselves as such and develop ways of pursuing common concerns and interests. Others come to view them as a separate group as well, and they acquire a common identity and position in the world, especially in a somewhat fluid society like our own. How separate the community becomes depends largely on what is needed to secure the benefits of that way of life for its members and on the attitude of the surrounding society toward the way of life to which it is dedicated. All this is simply the natural consequence of people adopting an ideal and way of life. It is the way, for example, that monastic communities developed historically out of collections of individuals who independently decided to abandon worldly ties and pursue a more holy life. How could such people fail to form their own communities?

# 18

# Objections

Most people want to avoid conflict and unpleasantness, so neighbors and onlookers usually incline to treat minority communities with forbearance, at least if those involved are orderly and productive and do not interfere with others. And from the standpoint of Catholic social teaching, close-knit local communities are a realization of subsidiarity, the principle of making life more participatory and building solidarity with those around us by carrying it on as locally as possible.

Even so, in spite of our age's commitment to self-determined identities, the idea of a coherent and distinctive Christian community puts many people off. Paradoxically, an age that makes everything a social construction finds separation from the social mainstream as alarming as men once found separation from God. If there is no natural law to live by, and man is defined by his appetites and arbitrary will, who knows what people who separate themselves from the social world inhabited by *New York Times* readers might do? When people in that world think of those who choose to be outsiders, they think of cultishness, various forms of abuse, and even terrorism.

## Turning inward

Some objections are mostly a matter of semantics. The idea of a distinct Christian community is now associated with the phrase "Benedict Option." "Benedict" sounds antiquarian, "Option" sounds like "optional," and the phrase as a whole suggests that we are all going to head for the hills. Rod Dreher, who invented the expression, is also known for the phrase "crunchy conservatism," which sounds like a post-hippy lifestyle choice for snooty rightists. Put it all together, and it sounds to many people—

rightly or not—like a self-indulgent escapist fantasy for bored middle-class people who do not want to deal with things they do not like to think about.

## The Church and the world

Other objections, some of them specifically religious, are more substantive. The Second Vatican Council called for greater openness to the world.[1] As Pope Saint Paul VI noted, the Council "felt the need ... almost to run after [the society in which the Church lives] in its rapid and continuous change."[2] The result, echoing the anti-transcendental trend of modern life, is that Catholics have been encouraged to put the secular world at the center of their concerns. That attitude, along with the Great Commission given the apostles to make disciples of all nations and the urge to do battle with social evils, leads many Catholics to view anything that suggests separation or seems reminiscent of "fortress" or "ghetto" Catholicism as a refusal to engage the world around us because it is stressful and might violate our supposed purity.

Conservative Catholics who take that view often find much of their Catholic identity in militancy. To separate from the world, they believe, is to give up the fight to defend the Church, spread the Good News, promote the true public good, and oppose the so-called culture of death. Catholics should focus on God and neighbor, not on themselves, and this means a combination of prayer and social engagement. There are also progressive Catholics who are appalled by the idea of specifically Catholic communities because they dislike the idea of Catholic identity. They see any separation from the world as turning away from other people, and against a great progressive movement toward justice in which Christ and humanity together overcome the rancor of social division through the universal inclusiveness of love. More pointedly, they see it as the sort of anti-Christian tribalism that led (they say) to the Inquisition and Crusades. As a result, they merge the demands of the Faith with those of secular progressivism, view racism, sexism, homophobia, and religious division as

---

1 *Gaudium et Spes*.
2 Conclusion of the II Vatican Council: Speech at the Last Public Session.

matters of deep religious concern, and welcome the weakening of traditional forms of identity and the boundaries of the Church, viewing this as the advent of a world in which, as Paul said in Galatians (3:28), "there is neither Jew nor Greek; there is neither bond nor free; there is neither male nor female."

Both groups see separation from the world to find God and save one's soul as self-centered and even self-contradictory. God made and loves the world—that is why He sacrificed Himself for it—and made us all members of each other. So if we want to know God, do His will, and save our souls, we should devote our efforts to living for others: accompanying them, supporting them, sharing their joys, sorrows, and struggles. More precisely, we should serve the poor, the cause of peace, the defense of life and marriage, or some other practical good. That, they believe, is how we build the Kingdom.

## Separation and engagement

Those who recognize a need for distinctiveness reject the progressive view of the Faith. They would likely say that Christianity transcends and transforms rather than eliminates distinctions, and that Paul's point in Galatians is that our connection through Christ trumps even basic and enduring social differences. It is as if someone said, "before God there is neither head surgeon nor scrub nurse." No one would view that as a call for radical democracy in the operating room. It would be a statement that no secular distinction, however necessary and justified, is of truly ultimate importance. And they might add that merging the Faith into secular progressivism deprives it of any specific function, and lends its support to a secularist movement that grows increasingly totalitarian yet cannot and will not deliver on its promises.

To conservatives, they would say that no one is proposing total disengagement from the world. Few are called to be monks. Other Catholics will be living in the world, doing its work, raising families, helping their neighbors, and dealing with all the practical difficulties involved in those things. And their ultimate social goal will be the same: a society in which the Church is free to do her work, and in which Christianity and natural law, rather than technology and progressive human rights, are the final standards by which social life and conduct in general are judged. The former standards, both agree, are adequate to man's nature and needs; the latter are not, but rather present an idealized image of a commercial and bureaucratic order.

What is proposed is separation to the degree needed for people to lead a distinctively Christian way of life. We cannot offer anything special to the world if we do not have something special that others have reason to want. The degree needed varies with circumstances and the particular people involved. It may be that the tendency toward radical rejection of natural law will weaken, so separation may be less needed in the future than it now seems to be. And in any event there are people who are able to thrive as Christians while totally immersed in an anti-Christian culture, so some people will not need separation anyway. But how many are so independent-minded? How many children, people struggling with temptation or bad habits, or even just everyday people subject to common human weaknesses? Those who are strong in their faith deserve praise, but the Church should be concerned about Christians who fall well short of perfection. So why not do something for them, who constitute the great majority of believers?

In any event, social action is not the heart of Christianity. Love of God comes before love of neighbor, contemplation before action, reforming ourselves before reforming the world. Nor is love of neighbor at bottom about activism. The dignity of man means that what is most important about people is how they carry on their lives, and we cannot do that for others. We can do what we can to diminish temptations, avert or mitigate evils, and promote good choices, but usually the most important thing we can do is to present an example of a good way of life. If others are not interested, we cannot force the matter. But even those who do not accept it can benefit from the example, since it can enlarge their understanding of what life can be, and that can change their world in subtle but powerful ways.

We should stay on good terms with others if we can, and when there is occasion to help we should do so. But love of neighbor is not the same as support and cooperation in all things, and current tendencies are making it harder for Catholics to join in many social institutions, practices, and causes. How will we be able to practice medicine if physicians are required to participate in abortion? Or participate in practical politics, if effective participation requires signing on to current orthodoxies? What we can do to act effectually in such matters we should, at least to the extent we are called to do so. Our duty as citizens, for example, requires us to use our vote realistically to promote the public good as we understand it in a setting that offers no choices that are not severely flawed. And the Catholic response to abortion—prayer, political action, public witness and argument, and support for mothers and marriage—provides an example of what can be done with regard to a concrete issue.

But political campaigns, however valuable, cannot be the focus of our social efforts. As discussed, it seems likely that we Catholics will have to put most of our social efforts into offering a good example, providing services directly and often informally, defending our freedom as Catholics, and presenting our views to the public—otherwise known as evangelization—through living as well as preaching. It would be useful, for example, to show that there is an alternative to projects like modern social democracy, which aims to serve man by integrating all social life into a system that refers to nothing beyond itself. Such an alternative would inevitably require living somewhat separately in community. In this and other ways, moderate separation would maintain our integrity amid political and social engagement.

Some will be in a position to engage with the larger society more directly and comprehensively: Saint Paul did not take the way of Saint Benedict. But not everyone is up to going out and taking on the world like Paul, who was unmarried, childless, specially commissioned, and unusually energetic, resourceful, devoted, resilient, and self-possessed. Some of us have enough trouble getting our own lives in order and keeping our children out of trouble, and need all the help we can get from those around us. So it is not surprising that Paul did not tell those he converted to act as he did.

## Benefits of monasticism

In any event, general objections to separation are too narrowly utilitarian. They ignore the variety of ways in which we affect each other, among which are prayer and contemplation. Catholics traditionally take such things seriously, and people who do not will be unable to see the full value of Benedict's way of life.

Christianity is not constant activity and engagement. Jesus started his ministry with thirty years of silence followed by forty days in the desert, and it was Judas who protested against wasting on a religious observance what could be given to the poor. The early Christians did not try to take over the synagogues, reform the Academy, lobby the emperor for social reform, or engage critically with the shows at the Theater of Marcellus. After the initial impulse, they—especially the laity—did not even do much overt evangelization. Instead, they concentrated on God and neighbor, lived their lives accordingly, and presented their views and way of life when called upon, converting others mostly by personal contact and the power of example. That was usually a very quiet matter, although at times their courage and charity profoundly impressed others, as when they refused to renounce the Faith when persecuted or risked their lives to help others during plagues.[3] In all these ways they presented an alternative to the mainstream that drew people because of what it was, and that changed the world.[4]

Something similar could be said about Saint Benedict, whose monasticism went far beyond anything proposed under the rubric of the "Benedict Option." He sought to enter the Kingdom of God by seeking solitude in the mountains, and by doing so he benefited the world immensely even by the most narrowly practical standards. His way made monasteries more stable and functional, improving the lives of monks and giving examples of ordered and productive community to a chaotic world. Those who pursued it provided charity and hospitality, preserved classi-

---

3 Kenneth Berding, "How Did Early Christians Respond to Plagues?"

4 Rodney Stark, *The Rise of Christianity: How the Obscure, Marginal Jesus Movement Became the Dominant Religious Force in the Western World in a Few Centuries*.

cal learning, developed better agricultural, industrial, and organizational techniques, and kept alive a nucleus of literate and civilized living in a time of barbarism and forgetfulness. So even apart from its specifically spiritual benefits and its institutional benefits to the Church, monasticism helped civilize all Europe. Put everything together, and what man of action ever did more to improve the world practically than Benedict did, even without intending to do so?

In any event, something like monasticism is necessary to Christianity, just as pure science concerned only with fundamental principles is necessary to applied science and technology. Its sharpness of focus points in a particularly striking way toward realities that should always guide the Church, and that reminder is absolutely necessary for Christians involved in secular life. The need is especially great when life is either too hard or too soft. When worldly life is brutal and disordered, and the Church is persecuted, she needs a place where she can catch her breath, collect her thoughts, and remember her ultimate goal. And when it is easy and prosperous, so that believers grow worldly and mediocre, and the Church grows compromised by her connections to worldly powers, she needs to have examples of heroic dedication to her fundamental vision. Otherwise she will forget who she and her members are.

Today we in the West have something of both problems. Intellectually, and at the level of informal human relationships, life grows inhuman, disordered, and anti-Christian. But it is physically soft for most people, certainly by historical standards, with endless opportunities for distraction, and powerful forces within the Church support assimilation to secular society. So there is reason to expect—to the extent such things can be predicted—a revival of monasticism. The Church needs the focus and opportunity for recollection it provides, and at some point more people will hear the need and answer the call. That will benefit all of us. Some see signs of such a development already, although as with all beginnings there is skepticism as to its value and how best to proceed.

## Exclusion

For many people the basic objection to close-knit Catholic community is the implication that Western life today is fundamentally misdirected: our ideals are degraded, our way of life increasingly nonfunctional, our experts ignorant of the things they most should know. Why should people who trust the modern world and favor its goal of universal this-worldly inclusion approve? And especially, why should the experts and other leaders who are guiding the effort do so? This objection is felt most strongly by secular people but also by progressive Catholics—as we have noted, there is a great deal of overlap in outlook.

## Objection

Those who lead public discussion believe that only recently, through the current emphasis on equality and human rights, have we begun to break free of the horrors of the past. More specifically, they believe that the radical weakening of traditional identities is a good thing because these limit human possibilities and force people into oppressive roles that make them miserable. Such people are naturally appalled by rejection of current tendencies in the name of tradition, religion, and natural law. They find it arbitrary, dangerous, and ill-intentioned. It reminds them of fascism.

Any sort of Benedict Option calls for a local community that is somehow set off from the world around it. That implies boundaries, exclusions, and restrictions on freedom that are at odds with the liberal order. These are now considered socially and morally outrageous. Respectable people in nineteenth-century America objected to Mormon polygamy, sometimes violently. Today they object to what they view as oppressive traditional structures. In an age in which the struggle against microaggressions is taken quite seriously and parents can lose custody of their children for "misgendering" them, oppression is defined broadly to include any hint of natural law or traditional standards regarding the family.

Strong local communities normally depend on traditional schemes of identity built around masculinity, femininity, the natural family, and religious and cultural heritage. An attempt to

*Objections*

increase community coherence and distinctiveness, however moderate and in line with Catholic moral and social doctrine, would thus be radically at odds with current social ideals. By current standards it would be sexist, patriarchal, homophobic, and transphobic. Nor would such communities escape accusations of racism. It is said that the most segregated hour in Christian America is eleven o'clock on Sunday morning. In even the most liberal denominations there is a stubborn tendency toward sorting on ethnic and racial lines, so much so that some mainstream commentators have come to think it is connected to positive things about congregational life.[5] This tendency can thus be expected at least to some extent within any movement toward closer local Catholic community. From the standpoint of today's public thought, however, it is intolerable.

## Response

Catholic communities are likely to reject complaints regarding family and sexual matters out of hand, due to the clear Catholic doctrine on such issues. The complaint about racism raises more difficulties for many. One response might be *tu quoque*: there are few enterprises of any sort that draw support equally from all racial groups. But more needs to be said. Current public thought makes community self-organization effectively illegitimate, since the connections people form on their own are never inclusive enough unless they treat inclusion as a goal that trumps all others—and rarely even then.[6]

In concept, cohesive local communities that are fundamental to the daily lives of their members might be held together simply by a common faith that is equally available to all. That principle held the earliest Christians described in Acts 2 together in a sort of primitive communism—even private property became irrele-

---

5 Martin Marty, "Taking the Unitarian Universalist Diversity Crisis Seriously."

6 In the nonprofit world, concentration on DEI (Diversity, Equity, and Inclusion) often prevents an organization from dealing with anything else. Ryan Grim, "Meltdowns Have Brought Progressive Advocacy Groups to a Standstill at a Critical Moment in World History."

vant. In such a setting, ethnic and cultural connections would also be irrelevant to the functioning of the community. So ideally Catholic communities might possess a degree of holiness that would make something similar possible. As a practical matter, though, such a situation would not last very long, any more than it did with the early Christians. We have weaknesses: that is one reason we need community. But a consequence of our weaknesses is that influences beyond the common love of God, like common history and culture, are generally needed to hold us together and keep us functional as communities. The issue is not "hate" or ethnic purity but practicality: it is easier for a community composed of families to function if there are common expectations and ways of doing things and thus a common culture.

And that is more than a crutch for weak people. Christianity values natural ties for their intrinsic positive aspects. At the beginning of his *Politics* Aristotle notes that human communities naturally arise out of the primordial community of the family. Correspondingly, it is easier for people to form communities if they already have family ties and similar connections—blood and marital relationships, common loyalties, ties of friendship, common history and culture, and so on. Such connections facilitate mutual trust and pursuit of common goods. Man is social, and he realizes himself through particulars—that is part of the meaning of the Incarnation. Christianity is neither Judaism, the faith of the Jewish people, nor Islam, which creates a single universal Muslim nation that in principle should replace all previous national communities. Instead, it accepts and even praises natural particularities such as family, nation, and culture. In *Centesimus Annus*, for example, Pope Saint John Paul II notes that one reason for the collapse of communism was its failure to accept the fundamental importance of national identity: "The struggle to defend work was spontaneously linked to the struggle for culture and for national rights."[7] And in *Dilecti Amici* he told young people, "we must do everything we can to accept this spiritual inheritance [of particular culture and history], to confirm it, maintain it and

7 Par. 24.

*Objections*

increase it."[8] Similar sentiments can be found in *Mater et Magistra*, by Pope Saint John XXIII, and *Summi Pontificatus*, by Pope Pius XII.

It seems entirely normal for a common religious effort to be aided by connections among participants that facilitate common efforts in general. And binding principles that might make up for a lack of natural or secular social connections have their own problems. Monastic vows impose a discipline that can help overcome differences, but they are not for everyone and do not suit family life. Religious cults rely on inadvisable means, such as isolation, thought control, and the mystique of the leader. Jim Jones' People's Temple, a spectacular example of a destructive cult, was admired for its multiracial egalitarianism long before it became famous for the mass suicide that brought it to an end. And we have seen the problems caused by the current secular attempt to create a universal technological society to which the particularities of nation, culture, and religion are irrelevant.

The testimony of the Church and common sense, then, is that we should accept the relevance of particular national, communal, and cultural connections to our ability to self-organize. Paul notes in Galatians that such connections are not the most important thing, but there are reasons they matter. Catholicism thus demands not that they be eliminated, but that they be properly subordinated.[9] So from a Catholic standpoint, it should not in general be objectionable if more people from one ethnic background than another are drawn to a particular Catholic community, or find the community congenial and stick with it.

## Lurking problems

Attempts to make local Catholic communities more distinct and cohesive should be guided by moderation and practical needs. If such efforts become common it seems unlikely many will go to unproductive extremes, since the ordinary laymen involved are likely to have so many other things to attend to. Their problem is more likely to be lukewarmness than extremism. But there can

---

8 Par. 11.
9 See Pope Pius XI, *Mit Brennender Sorge*.

be problems, as with everything human. The corrosive social tendencies that now make a certain degree of separation advisable seem likely to intensify. If that happens—and the future is unpredictable—successful communities are likely to become ever more at odds with the larger society and may drift toward what progressives would see as Christian tribalism. For an extreme example of what that can mean, consider the Middle East, where religion is seemingly fundamental to community life but often seems to descend into tribalism. The illustration is not pleasing, but every possible society has features that can lead to serious problems. That is why prudence is necessary in human affairs.

But a movement toward particularity now seems inevitable. The abstract simplicity of basic liberal principles means that they cannot be kept from going to extremes. Their continuing development breaks down the identities and connections and excludes from public life the goods that people live by. But life must go on; man is social and religious, he needs to know who he is, and if the only way he can live in a setting hospitable to what he holds dear is to weaken his loyalty toward an ever more content-free public order and turn toward something more particular, he will do so. If current centrifugal tendencies continue and we do not have Catholic community to counteract them we will have something else—very likely ethnic separatism, political and religious fanaticism, and gated communities with armed guards for the rich and gang-ridden slums for the poor. Instead of a Christian particularity that accepts ultimate loyalty toward something substantive and universal, and so has features that moderate it and prevent absolute communal egotism, we will have a particularity that rejects such loyalties and sees them as self-betrayal. And that would leave very little hope for a peaceful and humane world.

# 19

# Challenges

As Catholic communities try to survive and define themselves under increasingly unfavorable circumstances, they will have to deal with internal and external challenges. How severe these challenges become depends on future developments, but at this point they seem likely to be severe.

## Legal

Any movement toward stronger Catholic communities is bound to run into legal problems. A Catholic hospital would not offer "assistance in dying," a Catholic school would not teach the equality of all religions, and a gay Hmong atheist would not be as much at home in a setting influenced by traditional Catholicism as a conservative Irish Catholic who is married with eight children. How could such things be allowed in the new world now coming into view? It seems likely, then, that in the foreseeable future the Church's political efforts should focus on defending her freedom. More specifically, we will need to defend our right to live as we think best individually and in community, and to say what we believe to be true.

This will mean defending parental and conscience rights against politically correct compulsion: the right of small businessmen to run their businesses in accordance with their religious and moral standards, the right of parents to educate their children at home or send them to genuinely independent schools, and the liberty of the Church, which includes her freedom to proclaim her message and carry on her affairs as she sees fit. The First Amendment provides some protection, but it cannot be relied on. The rule of law is weakening in America, due to the disintegration of reason and the increasingly ideological and partisan nature of public life; and in any event the Constitution must be interpreted, and the intellectual background against which it is interpreted is changing. The freedom of the Church can be defended to some extent on the basis of the classical liberal conception of freedom, but liberal conceptions evolve. Classical liberalism is all but dead, and influential thinkers are becoming less committed to special protection for speech and religion. Both can be harmful, and they see nothing special about religion other than what they consider its irrationality,[1] and little reason to oppose censorship when their allies are solidly in control. The connection of Catholicism to natural law, and therefore to traditional sexual standards and understandings of identity, only makes matters worse. It is hard to overstate the fanaticism of current opposition to such things. So it seems likely that First Amendment protections will more and more be interpreted in a minimalist way.

That means we will have to engage in constant political action to prevent straightforward application of principles like inclusiveness that are now considered utterly compelling.[2] Even today, parents are losing custody of their children for refusal to cooperate in their supposed transition from one sex to the other. And many people are convinced it would advance freedom to require Catholic schools to make celebrating gay identity part of their fundamental mission. After all, if the normal and the perverse are put on the same level as equal exercises of liberal autonomy, how can the former be privileged?

So it seems we must become indigestible, refuse to cooperate, and insist on the correctness of our position and the right to do what is right. It will not be easy to do so. Catholics will have to know their convictions and why they hold them, and be ready to stand up and argue for them steadily and articulately in the face of opprobrium—and if necessary, be ready to suffer for them. A Church that cares about her faith, her people, and the world would strive to develop such qualities in her clergy, scholars, and

---

1 Christopher Shea, "Beyond Belief."
2 Consider, for example, the Equality Act and the U.S. bishops' response to it. CNA Daily News, "US Bishops: Equality Act Will Hurt More Than Help."

other faithful. And she would take special care to avoid undercutting the efforts of her advocates by blurring the clarity of her doctrine. Here again there is a great deal that needs to be done within the Church to provide true pastoral care.

## Social

Another challenge will be maintaining focus and coherence in a setting that tends to dissolve them. Catholic communities would most often arise gradually and organically, through the development of new habits and growth of new identities around parishes and among circles and networks of friends. A reading or prayer group or charitable project, or a parish with a particularly good priest and liturgy, might provide the initial seed. People might come and go, and some people would belong and others half-belong.

Many communities would stay like that, formally unstructured and reliant on the active commitment of their members. But many other communities are likely to feel a need for defined standards to support an outlook and way of life that is becoming ever more in opposition to that surrounding it. And the communities that remain more informal, as well as Catholics (who will likely remain the majority) who remain looser in their commitments, are likely to look to more dedicated communities to set a standard, as ordinary Catholics have looked to clergy and religious, the Protestant churches have looked to the Catholic Church, and the "God-fearers" of antiquity looked to the Jews who fully observed the Law.

The contemporary world is intrusive; it is hard to break with customary ways of doing things, and people tend to assimilate to their environment. The Church accepted the Greek and Roman classics because of what is good in them, but Netflix is not Homer, and the early Church also rejected a great deal of Roman popular culture. Can we imagine what her response would have been to cable TV, the Internet, smart phones, and social media? Saint Paul notes that "evil communications corrupt good manners" (1 Cor 15:33), and between electronics and the increasing importance in all spheres of large organizations committed to anti-Catholic understandings, we are now bathed in them. Under such circumstances, stability of commitment is likely to call more and more for community support as well as personal conviction and informal personal connections. So definite standards for engagement in mainstream social life are likely to emerge.

All sorts of questions need to be settled. Which popular entertainment is acceptable? What should be done about courtship and standards for marriage? And what should be done if someone violates them? A transition from personal choice and voluntary involvement to articulated group standards can be bumpy. Something is lost by it; opinions will differ on what is needed; enforcement is tricky, whether based on community sentiment or something more formal; and some people will drop out. It is easier to say you want a new way of life, especially in a loosely connected consumer society in which Christianity looks like one more lifestyle option, than do what is needed to make it a reality.

In the long run, though, stable and functional Christian community in an increasingly adverse environment requires recognized authority. Authority is always imperfectly exercised and often abused. Communities will have to exercise good sense if they find they need a more definite structure and standards,[3] aiming at stability and function rather than perfections that cannot be forced. It seems evident that the hierarchical Church will have to play a role to maintain perspective and objectivity. But that will require hierarchs to read the signs of the times and change what they do to accommodate new realities, something they have been slow to do. Not long ago, they were visibly concerned with all aspects of how Catholics lived, for example with regard to education, participation in non-Catholic political movements, and popular entertainment such as the movies. Catholics were forbidden to read certain books, or to take part in ecumenical worship. It will likely be necessary to revisit such matters.

Catholics will also have to make their life together attractive enough to be worth any necessary limitations. That partly depends on what is available elsewhere. Social disorder is debilitating, and an orderly way of life oriented toward basic human

---

[3] For discussion of the need for simplicity and moderation, see David Larson, "What Works When Making a Christian Community and What Doesn't."

goods has its own attractiveness. Most of us would rather live among people of generally upright life, and friendship and festivity spring eternal among socially minded people joined in the search for genuine higher goods. So it should not be difficult to find the way to something more rewarding than Facebook and Roku.

## Economic

We will likely struggle to find ways to make a living without offering a pinch of incense to Caesar. Paul could support himself as a tent-maker without violating or denying his beliefs. Today, employees of large companies and other institutions are increasingly unable to do so. The problem is acute because of the industrial organization of economic life and the scale and ambition of the modern state. The Roman state was tiny by today's standards, and there was no central authority to control how peasants, artisans, and shopkeepers managed their affairs. Christians did not pose an immediate practical problem, at least until they became numerous and influential enough to seem a threat to Diocletian's vision of a restored empire. So in spite of sporadic persecution Christians were mostly left alone to live as they chose and influence or persuade others to their way of life.

Our modern Caesars have far more ambition and resources, so they involve themselves in all aspects of life. Anti-discrimination laws make it impossible to give a business organization of any size a specifically Catholic identity, for example by preferring employees who accept Catholic principles. Instead, these laws effectively force large organizations to reduce the risk of lawsuits by promoting gender ideology and other anti-Catholic beliefs among their employees. So businesses that want to be Catholic will have to be small and mostly informal, perhaps taking the form of networks of independent contractors. Such an arrangement fits the emphasis on local and community life, but it creates complications. Perhaps Catholics will increasingly become plumbers, electricians, auto mechanics, and so on. The money is generally good, there is always a demand, and there seems less spiritual slavishness than in more bureaucratized occupations. The heresy hunters are always with us, and may eventually feel called upon to do something about the ability of "extremists" to find refuge in such occupations,[4] but we can only do our best.

We will also need to reduce our wants, emphasize mutual aid, and restore as much as we can of the practical functions of the home. That will reduce our need for money, and it can be educational as well as liberating. Wealth lets you be stupid, but thought and skill are needed to make a little go a long way. Specialization, the industrial system, and the cult of expertise are destroying the competence and self-government of individuals, families, and local communities. Home and family are the school of such things. Homeschooling makes the domestic economy far more serious. So do gardening, the arts of homemaking, home-based business, home repair and maintenance, and all the other ways people provide for their needs by engaging directly and practically with the world around them.

How far could that go? An industrial economy promotes the industrial outlook on life that is at the root of many of our problems. It seems that people would be better and happier if they could live once again in a non-industrial world of craftsmen, small farmers, and domestic economy, with technology controlled so that it becomes an adjunct to those things. That is the sort of thing G.K. Chesterton and Hilaire Belloc had in mind with their distributism. But distributism has never gone much of anywhere, even though many people love the idea and some have tried to put it into practice. The efficiencies of industrial organization are too tempting. But we will not be the first to deal with such problems. The Amish go to an extreme few will want to follow, but it might be possible to learn something from them. The Orthodox Jews and Mormons provide other models that may be helpful. The latter have managed to combine maintenance of intense communal life with effective evangelization. All demonstrate what can be done, and Catholics will find their own way if that is truly what they want. No doubt a great deal of trial and error will go into whatever they end up with, with different groups arriving at different accommodations.

---

4 See, for example, Daniel Greenfield, "National Association of Realtors Imposes Cancel Culture on 1.4 Million People."

## Educational

If sink-or-swim in an ocean of secularism is bad for ordinary Catholics, it is a thousand times worse for their children. Education inculcates an understanding of man, the world, and the purpose of life, so it necessarily has a religious aspect. State education educates children into the implicit religion of the state, and that is certainly not Catholicism. Why has Catholic education become less available than it was when Catholics were poorer? And why have so many Catholic schools become so dubiously Catholic? There are Catholic homeschoolers who would love to send their children to the Catholic school down the block but cannot in good conscience because the education on offer is not actually Catholic.

The Church needs once again to take seriously her responsibility for education. Until she does, she will continue to neglect an obvious pastoral duty—and a basic need to renew thought and culture, and make a more Catholic way of life readily available to ordinary people, will remain unaddressed. This cannot continue.

## Intellectual

Many of our current situation's roots are intellectual. We need to be able to respond effectively at that level, and cannot rely on other people to do so. So we need more intellectual interest on the part of ordinary Catholics, and more universities, publications, and other cultural institutions that are genuinely Catholic.

It seems likely we will become more able to do so in the coming years. The reasons are intellectual and cultural as well as specifically religious. Before the Second Vatican Council, many people complained about the narrowness of the Catholic ghetto. The idea seemed to be that the life of the world was going on much more outside the Church than within her, and the Church should throw open her doors and windows, let in the light and air, and go where the action is. That strategy failed to improve Catholic intellectual and cultural life, which has gone downhill together with the secular culture to which it was assimilating. It turns out that rejecting natural law, fudging distinctions, adopting a pragmatic attitude toward truth, and making choice the highest good do not promote true or productive thought.

People who care about truth are likely at some point to take such considerations to heart. If we are right that the Church has a better grip on reality than today's secular culture does, that is what will happen. Thought never remains still, and when it falls apart it eventually rebounds. After the decline of intellectual activity in Roman antiquity, it came back in the Church. Saint Augustine converted when the exhaustion of classical culture had made the Church the natural home for intellectual life. More recently, communist oppression and stupidity led to the achievements of samizdat literature, much of it inspired by Christianity. As the Soviet writer Ilya Ehrenburg noted, "You could cover the whole earth with asphalt, but sooner or later green grass would break through."

The early Middle Ages, with the radical disruptions brought on by the migrations of peoples, the rise of Islam, and political chaos, were another low point for thought. By Charlemagne's time, things had settled down enough for Alcuin to write:

> It may be that a new Athens will arise in France, and an Athens fairer than the old, for our Athens, ennobled by the teaching of Christ, will surpass the wisdom of the Academy. The old Athens had only the teachings of Plato to instruct it, yet even so it flourished by the seven liberal arts. But our Athens will be enriched by the gift of the Holy Spirit and will, therefore, surpass all the dignity of earthly wisdom.[5]

It took centuries, but that vision came to fruition in the intellectual and artistic culture of the High Middle Ages. Something of the sort may happen again, and there may someday be yet another Athens here in America. That is, of course, a distant prospect, and will doubtless require radical changes in intellectual life and social arrangements that we cannot now envision or do much to bring about. But we need to do what we can through recognition of principles higher than desire and success, withdrawal from the network of distractions that surrounds us, and

---

5 Quoted in Christopher Dawson, *Religion and the Rise of Western Culture: The Classic Study of Medieval Civilization*.

an overriding loyalty to institutions that are independent of market and state, reject utility, efficiency, and equality as supreme standards, and maintain an essential orientation toward the good, beautiful, and true. These institutions include Church, family, and the academy as traditionally conceived. Since they are independent and oriented toward goods that transcend money and power, they can offer a setting for disinterested consideration of basic issues, and give people a dignity and self-confidence that do not depend on career. That is why issues such as religious freedom, the nature and status of the family, and political correctness in the academy have been central to the culture wars.

Ordinary Catholics can help in several ways, for example by growing in the Faith, living in a Catholic manner, and cultivating their independence from an anti-Catholic world by disengaging from electronic media and instead studying history, pursuing literature, old books, and the arts, and reconnecting to sources of Catholic tradition like the Bible and the lives of the saints. But such voluntary and informal efforts have their limits. The Church needs to reestablish her intellectual independence, and in the long run independence requires authority. Catholic populism does not work. The discipline and stable efforts and relationships required for continuous coherent thought require the support of the institutional Church, so the Church hierarchy must play a role in any movement of reform and restoration.

In recent decades Catholic institutions have tended to assimilate to the world around them, which has made resistance to liberal modernity within Catholicism anti-institutional. This situation must change, and the leadership of the Church must once again pick up the torch of resistance and rebirth. The logic of the situation and the natural tendency of well-founded institutions to return to type make such a change inevitable, however much some ecclesiastical bureaucrats and even high-placed churchmen fight it.

# Spiritual

A Church that comes to be largely dependent on intensely Catholic local communities that are rather at odds with the larger society will be distant from wealth, power, prestige, and social position. It will thus be rather like the early Church. That will bring some benefits, increasing the commitment involved in membership and focusing attention on the Church's essential nature. Members will be members because they want what only the Church can provide: the presence of God and eternal life. But a more devoted Church will require overcoming stubborn ecclesiastical vices. She will, of course, have to reject the world as a standard. But doing so can mean treating ourselves as the standard. Pompous self-will is hard to root out of any organization that considers what it does important, and cultishness is hard to avoid in small self-selected ecclesial communities with an outlook at odds with the rest of society. What the Church will need to overcome these faults is what she always needs: sanctity. Sanctity requires the selflessness that sets us free and allows us to see reality, but it cannot be attained without daily self-denial. This sounds very difficult, a job for saints or at least those who seriously aspire to become such, but that is what will be needed in the coming years.[6]

In *The End of the Modern World*, written in Germany shortly after the Second World War, Fr Romano Guardini gave a relentlessly bleak account of the new age now upon us. He called for heroes who could combine the total devotion to the Faith of the saint with the absolute independence of the stoic from external circumstances. So far such people have not appeared. Quite the contrary—our human weaknesses, vanities, compromises, and self-indulgences seem only to get worse. But human nature, needs, and possibilities remain the same. These cannot be fulfilled in what society is becoming, so something must change. It seems that the way forward will have to include something like the course sketched out by Fr Guardini. We may not be up to carrying it very far; we can only do our best. For the rest, it seems we will need to trust a great deal in Providence.

---

6 This discussion of spiritual issues in the future Church draws on then-Father Joseph Ratzinger's 1969 address "What Will the Church Look Like in 2000?," printed in Joseph Cardinal Ratzinger, *Faith and the Future*.

## Gradual decay

Success is not always success in spiritual matters. As time passes, dedication and discipline flag. A community that starts by trying to do good is likely, if its way of life is successful, to end up doing well. And the more successful and enduring the community is, the more likely it is to take on tribal characteristics and rely too much on them for its continuation and self-understanding. There are no utopias and there is no way to avoid such tendencies completely. To the extent the Church and local churches become defined, distinctive, and autonomous, they become polities, and politics has a notorious tendency to become non-spiritual or worse. Even so, Catholics and others of good will must live with the world as it is and deal with its realities. There are dangers in every possible setting, and we can only do our best.

Life has ups and downs, and decadence often calls forth renewed sanctity. The Church's strength is that her traditions, sacraments, and doctrines preserve what she has to offer among flawed human beings even through the worst of times, so that when her members feel moved to rebuild they have memories and a structure to build upon. If success should become a problem we can deal with it then: sufficient unto the day is the evil thereof. Today our problems are very different.

# 20

# Outlook

We have considered the crisis of identity overwhelming the Western world and concluded that the problems leading to that crisis are so basic that they can only be fixed by way of what is likely to be a long and difficult road leading to the rebirth of Catholic civilization. These problems result from a weakening connection among life, thought, and reality, and they can be resolved only by restoring our grasp of the nature of things. That grasp is religious as well as natural—it must extend to the heights as well as the depths of being—and Catholics believe that its fullness can only be found within the Church.

Its restoration will require conversion of life and recapture of fundamental understandings of nature and reason that have a place for particular ties, stable identities, and transcendent commitments. Markets, bureaucracies, and arbitrary choice can no longer be all in all. The process will not be easy. It will have to start with relatively few devoted people, spread to those who are ready for it, and then ultimately, if the understandings are indeed correct and those who adhere to them true to their calling, transform the world.

Liberal modernity claims to be based on freedom and equality, but it attempts to turn social life into an industrial process under detailed expert supervision and control. The results include disruption of local, non-market, and non-bureaucratic institutions, and of traditional identities and patterns of life along with them. That suppresses the things people actually live by, their ability to live in accordance with nature and reason, and even their understanding of who they are. But to oppose current trends appears insane to most educated people today. Opposition means saying experts are ignorant, stereotypes and discrimination are often good, and people ought to rely on non-liberal institutions like family, religion, and particular inherited community that have been radically weakened and socially discredited. Since opposition depends on accepting distinctions that are not relevant to bureaucracies and global markets, it is said to involve hating people who are different simply because they are different.

But the general judgment of humanity throughout the ages tells us that it is today's progressives who are insane. They are ignoring basic aspects of human life, and the resulting denial of obvious distinctions and patterns means they have lost touch with reality. Human life is not technological. We are neither gods nor machines, and we cannot make our world, decide for ourselves who we are, or transform ourselves in ways that ignore history and natural design. To understand life we must see ourselves as situated through our origins and physical makeup, through family, community, and culture, and through higher principles that order our world and give it meaning. All these things help form our understanding of who we are, but liberal modernity does not allow us to act on this because it insists that we define those things for ourselves and invent our own identity. That, of course, cannot work. How can my identity—what I am—be something I am free to make up as I go along? What good can such a fabricated identity do for me? How can it give me an orientation in the world and establish my connections to others by telling them what to make of me? And if I make up my own identity, who is the "I" that makes it up and on what basis can it do so?

The task of those who see what is happening is to survive the current situation, stay in touch with fundamental realities, defend and carry forward as much sanity and civilization as possible, propagate the truth as opportunity offers, and eventually prevail as liberalism, modernity, and post-modernity destroy themselves.

Technological ways of thinking are often useful, but they cannot define a human world, and must accept their place within a world ordered by nature, history, and tradition. And that world must itself be understood as part of something larger still, a cosmic order that in some way is ordered toward good. Otherwise, nature, history, tradition, and identity become brute facts the world has thrust upon us, and we will inevitably resist and try to overcome them. That will send us back to the absolute dominion of technological ways of thinking. In the long run, accepting a world we do not dominate requires supernatural faith. Without it there is no escape from the view that for us man must be the measure, his desires the standard, his truth and identity what he decides for himself, and everything that might restrict him an enemy to be destroyed. If there is no God then man becomes God. We cannot carry the load, so the result is catastrophe.

Stable and effective supernatural faith requires an institution responsible for preserving it and passing it down. It is the Church, in spite of her human mediocrity and corruption, that connects us to a point outside the world from which it can be understood and moved. And she provides a community worthy of supreme loyalty that fosters tradition, recognizes natural law, supports natural and rational understandings of identity, embodies transcendent standards acceptable to reason, and possesses a structure of authority capable of resolving make-or-break issues. Even politically, *extra ecclesiam nulla salus*. These things can be obscured, but they cannot be lost. For two thousand years they have repeatedly brought the Church back from what seemed certain death. And even from a human standpoint, by establishing a pattern that works durably they are perpetually leading her to revert to type.

So in spite of the power of our opponents, and our weakness and corruption, we have everything we need to prevail. To recognize that God is at the center of all things is to dissolve the fictitious anti-world of liberal modernity and to be able once again to know who we are and what we are for. That recognition is a task for a lifetime, but what has been done before can be done again. To that end the Church and her members need to turn away from the forces of dissolution, reform themselves, and hold to what is true. They will eventually find their way to what is needed if that is what they want: seek and ye shall find. Even now they are doing so. Beyond the mediocrity and corruption in the Church there are signs of new life—some evident, some despised and rejected, some invisible to people who spend too much time online or reading official pronouncements, some hidden from everyone. "The kingdom of God," we are told, "cometh not with observation" (Lk. 17:20).

The immediate outlook, humanly speaking, is bad. The destruction of non-liberal institutions and of thought itself make it difficult to fight liberal modernity effectively or even remember who we are or what we are fighting for. But *naturam expellas furca, tamen usque recuret*: you may drive nature out with a pitchfork, but she will keep coming back. Life returns; human beings remain human, and nature, history, tradition, religion, and identity remain fundamental to how they live and understand themselves. The attempt to render these things irrelevant through technology cannot succeed. Groups as different as the Amish and Mormons have been able to thrive in America while maintaining their distinctiveness, and we can do the same. What works for us will no doubt evolve through trial and error, with different people finding different solutions. Saint Benedict, Saint Paul, and the congregations Paul established present varied forms of the Christian life, and the history of the Faith presents many others. We have as many models as we need if we will look and learn.

But what then? The future belongs to those who accept the truth about man and the nature of things. A great civilization can be disrupted, but when the fit passes it returns to type if its principles are adequate to human life. Christians believe Christianity is the way, and if they are right truth itself will fight for them. If people manage to live well in an increasingly disordered world, what they stand for will prevail. So if Christian civilization is worth saving, it can be saved. It is up to us. Our political hope is for a world in which Christianity, like science and liberal human rights today, is the final standard by which society and institutions are judged. That goal may seem very distant, but technocratic liberalism will not last; there is no rule for what comes next, and what works wins. In a time of increasingly radical disorder the outlook and way of life that best fits human needs, nature, and aspirations will have an advantage. So even from a purely natural perspective, the Church and her vision are likely to prevail over her modern opponents.

However alarming trends may be, we should remember that evils conflict with each other, so we are not going to get all of them at once. Some may even help us maintain our freedom as Catholics. The inefficiency, irrationality, and corruption produced by an increasingly incoherent public culture will make enforcement of official principles hit-or-miss and generate a demand for something better among ordinary people. And the demographic diversity that seems almost certain to continue increasing in a globalized age will disrupt social connections and make free government ever more difficult, but it will also bring a growing presence throughout the West of people who are not Western liberals[1] and want to live in their own way, and so make it more difficult to enforce conformity.

One outlook and way of life replaces another when those who reject the established one start debunking it and promoting and living by another that seems better. That is how liberationist views won in the 1960s after a long history in which they were despised and often suppressed. Eventually persistence, boldness, the disarray of their opponents, and a conviction of their obvious correctness carried the day. To deal with the present situation we need to do what both our opponents and our ancestors in the Faith did: articulate, justify, and above all live by our basic understandings. Our opponents think of the world as a free field for the human will; we think of it as an ordered moral cosmos in which we all have a part. Which view is likely to yield better results in the long run?

We therefore have good grounds for hope. Progressivism has the support of all established institutions, but it is a consequence of intellectual and spiritual errors that are visibly refuting themselves and depend on the support of institutions they cannot sustain in the long run. That is why our rulers, in spite of their stated commitment to free thought and expression, feel compelled to suppress contrary views and subject us to nonstop propaganda. The struggle will of course be difficult, and we must avail ourselves of all legitimate aids. Those horrified by liberal modernity have no vehicle for their opposition but the Barque of Peter. To

---

[1] Consider, for example, the use of "white left" as a Chinese Internet insult. Chenchen Zhang, "The Curious Rise of the 'White Left' as a Chinese Internet Insult."

stand up to modernity and bring about a different way of life, a renewed grasp of basic realities must take definite institutional and dogmatic form. Who but the Church can give it that form?

Insanity can be enormously destructive until it destroys itself, so there are going to be storms and losses on the way, and the Church needs to be ready for them. I hope that this book has clarified the issues and suggested ways Catholics can help her do so. And I pray that the pastors of the Church, without whom little can ultimately be achieved, will remember who they are, and receive the wisdom and courage they need for the difficult times now before us.

# Bibliography

Aitkenhead, Decca. "Rachel Dolezal: 'I'm Not Going to Stoop and Apologise and Grovel.'" *The Guardian: US News*, February 25, 2017. https://www.theguardian.com/us-news/2017/feb/25/rachel-dolezal-not-going-stoop-apologise-grovel.

Alexander, Scott. "What Caused the 2020 Homicide Spike?" *Astral Codex Ten*, June 28, 2022.

Anderson, Ryan. "Sex Reassignment Doesn't Work. Here Is the Evidence." *The Heritage Foundation*. www.heritage.org/gender/commentary/sex-reassignment-doesnt-work-here-the-evidence.

Appiah, Kwame Anthony. "There Is No Such Thing as Western Civilisation." *The Guardian*, November 9, 2016.

Bader, Hans. "*Washington Post* Leaves False Impression About the Crime Rate." *Liberty Unyielding*, November 17, 2020.

Ball, Molly. "The Secret History of the Shadow Campaign That Saved the 2020 Election." *Time*, February 4, 2021.

Benedict XVI, Pope. Apostolic Journey to Brazil: Inaugural Session of the Fifth General Conference of the Bishops of Latin America and the Caribbean at the Conference Hall of the Shrine of Aparecida, May 13, 2007.

Berding, Kenneth. "How Did Early Christians Respond to Plagues?" *The Good Book Blog*, March 16, 2020. www.biola.edu/blogs/good-book-blog/2020/how-did-early-christians-respond-to-plagues.

Berger, Eric. "English Linked to Promiscuity in Hispanic Teens." *Houston Chronicle*, March 8, 2005.

Björkenstam, Charlotte, Gunnar Andersson, Christina Dalman, Susan Cochran, and Kyriaki Kosidou. "Suicide in Married Couples in Sweden: Is the Risk Greater in Same-Sex Couples?" *European Journal of Epidemiology* 31, no. 7 (July 2016): 685–90. doi.org/10.1007/s10654-016-0154-6.

## Bibliography

Bond, Paul. "Nearly 40 Percent of U.S. Gen Zs, 30 Percent of Young Christians Identify as LGBTQ, Poll Shows." *Newsweek*, October 20, 2021.

Breslau, Joshua, Guilherme Borges, Naomi Saito, Daniel J. Tancredi, Corina Benjet, Ladson Hinton, Kenneth S. Kendler, et al. "Migration from Mexico to the United States and Conduct Disorder: A Cross-National Study." *Archives of General Psychiatry* 68, no. 12 (December 2011): 1284–93. doi.org/10.1001/archgenpsychiatry.2011.140.

Catholic News Agency. "US Bishops: Equality Act Will Hurt More Than Help." *Catholic World Report*, March 20, 2019.

Chu, Johan S.G., and James A. Evans. "Slowed Canonical Progress in Large Fields of Science." *Proceedings of the National Academy of Sciences* 118, no. 41 (October 2021): e2021636118. doi.org/10.1073/pnas.2021636118.

Confucius. *The Great Learning*. Translated by James Legge. classics.mit.edu/Confucius/learning.html.

Dalrymple, Theodore. *Life at the Bottom: The Worldview That Makes the Underclass*. Chicago: Ivan R. Dee, 2003.

Dawson, Christopher. *Religion and the Rise of Western Culture: The Classic Study of Medieval Civilization*. New York: Image, 1991.

Dreher, Rod. *The Benedict Option: A Strategy for Christians in a Post-Christian Nation*. New York: Sentinel, 2017.

Eberstadt, Mary. *Adam and Eve after the Pill: Paradoxes of the Sexual Revolution*. San Francisco: Ignatius Press, 2012.

———. *Primal Screams: How the Sexual Revolution Created Identity Politics*. West Conshohocken, PA: Templeton, 2019.

Ellul, Jacques. *Propaganda: The Formation of Men's Attitudes*. New York: Knopf, 1968.

Eltagouri, Marwa. "Jeff Sessions Spoke of the 'Anglo-American Heritage of Law Enforcement.' Here's What That Means." *Washington Post*, February 12, 2018.

Evon, Dan. "New NYC Laws Prohibit Discrimination against Transgender Community." *Snopes*, December 28, 2015. www.snopes.com/fact-check/transgender-pronouns-fine-nyc.

Fagan, Patrick. "How U.N. Conventions on Women's and Children's Rights Undermine Family, Religion, and Sovereignty." Heritage Foundation, February 5, 2001. www.heritage.org/

global-politics / report / executive-summary-how-un-conventi ons-womens-and-childrens-rights-undermine.

Francis, Pope. *Amoris Laetitia*. 2016.

Garrett, Shaylyn Romney, and Robert D. Putnam. "Why Did Racial Progress Stall in America?" *The New York Times*, December 4, 2020.

Gilley, Bruce. *The Last Imperialist: Sir Alan Burns's Epic Defense of the British Empire*. Washington, DC: Regnery Gateway, 2021.

Greenfield, Daniel. "National Association of Realtors Imposes Cancel Culture on 1.4 Million People." *Front Page Magazine*, November 30, 2020. www.frontpagemag.com/fpm/2020/11/national-association-realtors-imposes-cancel-daniel-greenfield.

Grim, Ryan. "Meltdowns Have Brought Progressive Advocacy Groups to a Standstill at a Critical Moment in World History." *The Intercept*, June 13, 2022. https://theintercept.com/2022/06/13/progressive-organizing-infighting-callout-culture.

Guardini, Romano. *The End of the Modern World*. Wilmington, DE: Intercollegiate Studies Institute, 1998.

Hamby, Peter. "Baseball? Coachella? Handshakes? Tinder? Anthony Fauci on the New Rules of Living with Coronavirus." *Vanity Fair*, April 2020.

Hannah-Jones, Nikole, et al. "The 1619 Project." *The New York Times*, August 14, 2019.

Harvey, Josephine. "British Ex-Cop Jailed After Posting Racist Memes Mocking George Floyd's Death." *HuffPost*, June 15, 2022. www.huffpost.com/entry/former-british-cop-james-aa tts-jailed-racist-posts_n_62a946bfe4b06594c1cf6220.

Heilman, Uriel. "Pew Survey of U.S. Jews: Soaring Intermarriage, Assimilation Rates." *Jewish Telegraphic Agency*, October 1, 2013.

Helfand, Duke. "A Formula for Failure in L.A. Schools." *Los Angeles Times*, January 30, 2006.

Hemingway, Mollie. *Rigged: How the Media, Big Tech, and the Democrats Seized Our Elections*. Washington: Regnery, 2021.

Hobbes, Thomas. *Leviathan*. Ottawa: East India Publishing Company, 2021.

Ignatiev, Noel. *How the Irish Became White*. New York: Routledge, 1995.

Jaschik, Scott. "College Board Will Not Make Public AP Data by

Race." *Inside Higher Ed*, July 11, 2022. www.insidehighered.com/quicktakes/2022/07/11/college-board-will-not-make-public-ap-data-race.

Jégo, Yves. "Emmanuel Macron et le reniement de la culture française." *Le Figaro*, February 6, 2017.

John XXIII, Pope. *Mater et Magistra*. 1961.

John Paul II, Pope. *Dilecti Amici*. 1985.

———. *Centesimus Annus*. 1991.

Jones, Jeffrey M. "LGBT Identification in U.S. Ticks up to 7.1%." *Gallup*, February 17, 2022. news.gallup.com/poll/389792/lgbt-identification-ticks-up.aspx.

Jussim, Lee. *Social Perception and Social Reality: Why Accuracy Dominates Bias and Self-Fulfilling Prophecy*. New York: Oxford University Press, 2012.

Jussim, Lee, Clark R. McCauley, and Yueh-Ting Lee, eds. *Stereotype Accuracy: Toward Appreciating Group Differences*. American Psychological Association, 1995.

Kalb, James. *Against Inclusiveness: How the Diversity Regime Is Flattening America and the West and What to Do About It*. Brooklyn, NY: Angelico Press, 2013.

———. *The Tyranny of Liberalism: Understanding and Overcoming Administered Freedom, Inquisitorial Tolerance, and Equality by Command*. Wilmington, DE: ISI Books, 2008.

Katz, Roberta, Sarah Ogilvie, Jane Shaw, and Linda Woodhead. *Gen Z, Explained: The Art of Living in a Digital Age*. Chicago and London: University of Chicago Press, 2021.

Kelly, Julie, and Lee Smith. *January 6: How Democrats Used the Capitol Protest to Launch a War on Terror Against the Political Right*. New York: Bombardier Books, 2022.

Kendi, Ibram X. "There's Something Wrong with the Exam School Tests—Not with Black and Latinx Children." *Boston Globe*, October 22, 2020.

Kochenov, Dimitry. "Why We Shall Abolish Citizenship." *Review of Democracy*, December 2021.

Kolata, Gina, and Sabrina Tavernise. "It's Not Just Poor White People Driving a Decline in Life Expectancy." *The New York Times*, November 27, 2019.

Kruse, Michael. "What Do You Do If a Red State Moves to You?"

*Politico*, January/February 2017.

Kurth, Torsten, Clemens Möller, Jan-Frederik Jerratsch, Bianca Adolphs, Gerd Wübbels, and Decker Walker. "Reviving Agricultural Innovation in Seeds and Crop Protection." *BCG*, February 24, 2020. www.bcg.com/publications/2020/reviving-agricultural-innovation-seeds-crop-protection.

Larson, David. "What Works When Making a Christian Community and What Doesn't." *Crisis*, December 21, 2021. www.crisismagazine.com/2021/what-makes-a-christian-community-work-and-what-doesnt.

Liebeskind, Benjamin. "Einstein in Athens." *The New Atlantis*, no. 59. Summer 2019: 78–90.

Mac Donald, Heather. "The Corruption of Medicine." *City Journal*, Summer 2022. www.city-journal.org/the-corruption-of-medicine.

———. "The Guardians in Retreat." *City Journal*, Winter 2022. www.city-journal.org/art-institute-of-chicago-redefines-its-purpose-as-antiracism.

———. "The Revolution Comes to Juilliard." *City Journal*, May 23, 2021. www.city-journal.org/racial-hysteria-is-consuming-juilliard.

———. "Woke Science Is an Experiment Certain to Fail." *Wall Street Journal*, September 24, 2020.

Malone, Kelly. "Medically Assisted Deaths Could Save Millions in Health Care Spending: Report." *CBC*, January 23, 2017. www.cbc.ca/news/canada/manitoba/medically-assisted-death-could-save-millions-1.3947481.

Martin, James. *Building a Bridge: How the Catholic Church and the LGBT Community Can Enter into a Relationship of Respect, Compassion, and Sensitivity.* Revised, Expanded edition. HarperOne, 2018.

Marty, Martin. "Taking the Unitarian Universalist Diversity Crisis Seriously." *Sightings*, May 15, 2017. https://divinity.uchicago.edu/sightings/taking-unitarian-universalist-diversity-crisis-seriously.

McCoy, Brandon. "Closing the Racial Achievement Gap." *City Journal*, November 13, 2020. www.city-journal.org/proposition-16-defeat-closing-racial-achievement-gap.

## Bibliography

Miller, Cassie. "SPLC Poll Finds Substantial Support for 'Great Replacement' Theory and Other Hard-Right Ideas." *Southern Poverty Law Center*, June 1, 2022. https://www.splcenter.org/news/2022/06/01/poll-finds-support-great-replacement-hard-right-ideas.

Murray, Charles. *Coming Apart: The State of White America, 1960–2010*. Crown Forum, 2012.

Nisbet, Robert. *The Quest for Community: A Study in the Ethics of Order and Freedom*. Wilmington, DE: Intercollegiate Studies Institute, 2010.

Norman, Kajsa. "A Very Swedish Election." *Hurst*, September 14, 2018. www.hurstpublishers.com/a-very-swedish-election.

Packer, George. "When the Culture War Comes for the Kids." *The Atlantic*, October 2019.

Paul VI, Pope. Conclusion of the II Vatican Council: Speech at the Last Public Session. December 7, 1965.

Pius XI, Pope. *Mit Brennender Sorge*. 1937.

Pius XII, Pope. *Summi Pontificatus*. 1939.

Planned Parenthood of Southeastern Pa. v. Casey. 505 U.S. 833, 1992.

Putnam, Robert D. "E Pluribus Unum: Diversity and Community in the Twenty-first Century." *Scandinavian Political Studies* 30, no. 2 (June 2007): 137–74.

Ratzinger, Joseph Cardinal. *Faith and the Future*. San Francisco: Ignatius Press, 2009.

Reilly, Wilfred. Tweet, August 21, 2022. twitter.com/wil_da_beast630/status/1561447840978993152.

Reilly, Wilfred, Robert Maranto, and Patrick Wolf. "Did Black Lives Matter Save Black Lives?" *Commentary*, September 2022. www.commentary.org/articles/wilfred-reilly/did-black-lives-matter-save-black-lives.

Reno, R. R. *Return of the Strong Gods: Nationalism, Populism, and the Future of the West*. Washington, DC: Gateway Editions, 2019.

Robinson, Carol Jackson. *The Perverse Generation*. 3rd edition. Waterloo, ON: Arouca Press, 2021.

Rosenberg, Nathan. "Adam Smith on the Division of Labour: Two Views or One?" *Economica* 32, no. 126 (1965): 127–39.

Rufo, Christopher F. "Department of Homeland Security Training on 'Microinequities.'" *Rumor Mill News*, August 14, 2020. www.rumormillnews.com/cgi-bin/archive2.cgi/noframes/read/152429.

Rutz, David. "46 Times President Obama Told Americans 'That's Not Who We Are.'" *Washington Free Beacon*, November 30, 2015.

Schmitt, David P., Anu Realo, Martin Voracek, and Jüri Allik. "Why Can't a Man Be More Like a Woman? Sex Differences in Big Five Personality Traits Across 55 Cultures." *Journal of Personality and Social Psychology* 94, no. 1 (January 2008): 168–82. https://doi.org/10.1037/0022-3514.94.1.168.

Second Vatican Council. *Gaudium et Spes*. 1965.

Shea, Christopher. "Beyond Belief." *The Chronicle of Higher Education*, June 9, 2014.

Shrier, Abigail. *Irreversible Damage: The Transgender Craze Seducing Our Daughters*. Washington, DC: Regnery, 2020.

Sky News. "Black Murder Victims and Suspects: London v. UK." July 25, 2018. news.sky.com/story/black-murder-victims-and-suspects-london-v-uk-11443656.

Smith, Adam. *An Inquiry into the Nature and Causes of the Wealth of Nations*. 1776.

Smith, Steve. "Gender Reassignment Surgery Is Now Available to Oregon Minors without Parental Consent." *Medical Daily*, July 13, 2015. www.medicaldaily.com/gender-reassignment-surgery-now-available-oregon-minors-without-parental-consent-34267.

Spadaro, Antonio. "The Pontiff Meets the Jesuits of Mozambique and Madagascar." *La Civiltà Cattolica*, September 26, 2019.

Spadaro, Antonio, and Marcelo Figueroa. "Evangelical Fundamentalism and Catholic Integralism in the USA: A Surprising Ecumenism." *La Civiltà Cattolica*, July 13, 2017.

Stark, Rodney. *The Rise of Christianity: How the Obscure, Marginal Jesus Movement Became the Dominant Religious Force in the Western World in a Few Centuries*. San Francisco: HarperSanFrancisco, 1997.

Stoll, Ira. "List of People Canceled in Post-George-Floyd Antiracism Purges." *The Future of Capitalism*, June 11, 2020. www.futureofcapitalism.com/2020/06/list-of-people-canceled-in-post-george-floyd.

## Bibliography

Talbott, Stephen L. "Recovering the Organism." *The New Atlantis*, Fall 2010. www.thenewatlantis.com/publications/the-unbearable-wholeness-of-beings.

Tavernise, Sabrina. "Life Expectancy for Less Educated Whites in U.S. Is Shrinking." *The New York Times*, September 20, 2012.

United States v. Windsor, 570 U.S. 744 (2013).

"US Proposal for Defining Gender Has No Basis in Science." *Nature* 563, no. 7729 (October 2018): 5. doi.org/10.1038/d41586-018-07238-8.

Various signatories. "Against the Dead Consensus." *First Things*. www.firstthings.com/web-exclusives/2019/03/against-the-dead-consensus, March 21, 2019.

———. "Open Letter Against the New Nationalism." *Commonweal Magazine*, August 19, 2019. www.commonwealmagazine.org/open-letter-against-new-nationalism.

Vogt, Bailey. "NYC Bans Calling Someone an 'Illegal Alien' or Threatening to Contact ICE." *The Washington Times*, September 26, 2019.

Whitney, Karl. "Why Andy Martin, Documenter of a Changing Sunderland, Has Left His City." *The Guardian*, December 21, 2016.

Wolfe, Raymond. "World Economic Forum Head's Prediction of Microchips 'in Our Brains' Is Coming True, Thanks to Big Tech." *LifeSiteNews*, July 19, 2021.

Zaimov, Stoyan. "4 in 10 Americans Say Gender Is Not Determined at Birth: Survey." *Christian Post*, November 10, 2017.

Zhang, Chenchen. "The Curious Rise of the 'White Left' as a Chinese Internet Insult." *Hong Kong Free Press*, May 11, 2017.

Made in United States
North Haven, CT
29 July 2023